Collins

AQA GCSE 9-1

Combined Science Trilogy Foundation

Ian Honeysett, Sam Holyman and Ed Walsh

Exam Skills and **Practice**

How to use this book

This Exam Skills and Practice book puts the spotlight on the different types of command word - the instructional word or phrase in a question - you can expect to find in your GCSE papers. Each section has worked examples and lots of timed practice to help build your exam technique.

Top Tips offer nuggets of information to keep in mind when answering each type of question.

Scan the **QR code** to test your understanding of the command word and see a worked solution to the example question on that page.

Each question shows the paper **P1** **P2**, the part of the specification and grade range you are working at. Look out for maths skills 🔢 and practical skills 🔬 being tested.

Complete the example to take the next step in your practice. Parts of the workings and/or answers are given for you to finish. Helpful hints also steer you in the right direction.

Each **command word** is defined in easy-to-understand language.

Example questions show the command words in context. Use the QR code to access worked video solutions and commentary for them.

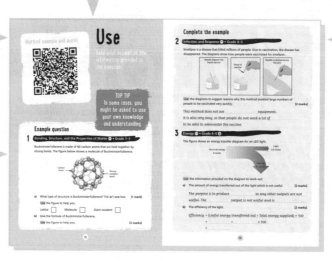

Exam practice questions enable you to delve deeper into each command word across a range of topics and grade levels. There is a target time for doing these at exam speed.

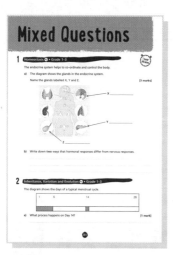

Mixed questions help to refine your exam skills with practice that recaps a variety of the command words.

An **index of topics** enables you to quickly find questions within the book from particular parts of the AQA GCSE specification.

Answers are given at the back of the book so that you can check and mark your own work.

Contents

Revise by command word!

Choose

Select your answer from a list of alternatives. These questions are usually targeted at lower grades as they give you a choice of answers.

Worked example and more!

TOP TIP
Use the options given, not your own words.

Example question

1 Cell Biology **P1** • Grade 1–3

This question is about animal cells. Which part of an animal cell carries out each function?

Choose answers from the box. **[3 marks]**

| cell membrane | cytoplasm | nucleus | mitochondria | ribosomes |

Contains the genetic material of the cell ....

Controls which substances enter or leave the cell ....

The site where proteins are made in the cell ....

Complete the example

2 Chemical Changes P1 • Grade 1–3

Complete the sentences.

Choose answers from the box.   [3 marks]

| chemical | oxidation | oxygen | reduction | respiration |

Chemical reactions happen when a new substance is made.

.... is an example of a chemical reaction where a substance

gains ....

3 Waves P2 • Grade 1–3

Complete the sentences.

Choose answers from the box.   [2 marks]

| Light | Infrared | Sound | Radio |

Infrared waves are used in electrical heaters and for cooking.

.... waves are longitudinal waves.

Exam practice questions

1 Homeostasis and Response P2 • Grade 1–3

Human reproduction is controlled by different hormones.

Which hormone controls each process in reproduction?

Choose the hormones from the box.   [3 marks]

| follicle stimulating hormone | luteinising hormone | oestrogen | progesterone |

The repair of the uterus lining after menstruation ....

The maturing of an egg in the ovary ....

The release of an egg from the ovary ....

2 Bioenergetics ℗1 • Grade 1–3

Photosynthesis produces glucose. This glucose is then converted to other substances that are needed by the plant.

Complete the two sentences about these conversions.

Choose the substances from the box.   **[2 marks]**

| amino acids | cellulose | fat | starch |

Glucose may be converted to _____ to strengthen cell walls.

It may also be converted to _____ for protein synthesis.

3 Ecology ℗2 • Grade 1–3

The diagram shows the carbon cycle.

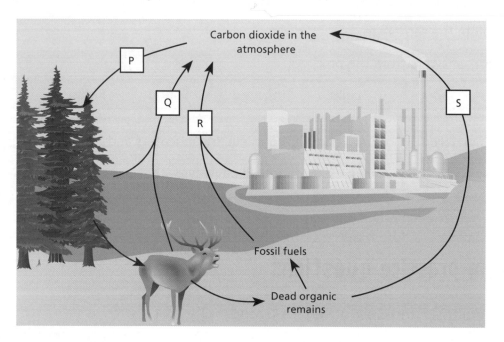

Identify processes P, Q, R and S.

Choose answers from the box.   **[4 marks]**

| combustion | decomposition | excretion | photosynthesis | respiration |

P = _____

Q = _____

R = _____

S = _____

Substances can change state when they are heated or cooled.

The figure below shows the changes of state.

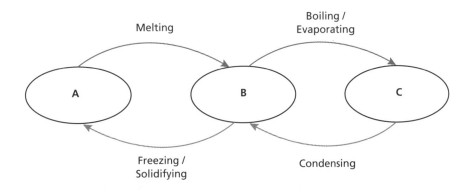

What do labels A, B and C represent?

Choose answers from the box.   **[3 marks]**

alloy	gas	liquid	solid

A = ...

B = ...

C = ...

5 **Chemical Analysis** ⓟ⒉ • Grade 1–3 ⓐ

In the electrolysis of sodium chloride solution, NaCl(aq), bubbles were seen at each electrode. Both gases were collected and tested.

Complete the sentences.

Choose answers from the box.   **[2 marks]**

carbon dioxide	chlorine	hydrogen	oxygen

The gas collected from the anode changed damp litmus paper white, so the gas was

....

The gas collected from the cathode burned rapidly with a pop sound, so the gas was

....

6 Chemical Changes ⓟ₁ • Grade 4–5 ⊖

A student can make a pure, dry sample of copper(II) sulfate by reacting copper(II) oxide.

Complete the sentences to explain the steps in the practical.

Choose the answers from the box.   **[4 marks]**

boiling	condensing	decrease	evaporating	excess
increase	filtrate	limiting	residue	

Sulfuric acid is heated up to .... the rate of reaction. As the

sulfuric acid is the .... reagent, the reaction mixture is filtered

to remove the .... copper(II) oxide.

The copper(II) sulfate crystals are obtained from the filtrate by

.... the water.

7 Chemistry of the Atmosphere ⓟ₂ • Grade 4–5

For 200 million years, the proportions of different gases in the atmosphere have been much the same as they are today.

The figure below is a pie chart which shows the composition of dry air.

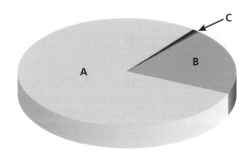

What do labels A, B and C represent?

Choose answers from the box.   **[3 marks]**

hydrogen	nitrogen	oxygen	water
carbon dioxide	oxygen	chlorine	

A = ...

B = ...

C = ...

8 Forces P2 • Grade 4–5 🔳

This question is about motion.

Complete the sentence.

Choose the answer from the box.   [1 mark]

| 7750 N | 8500 N | 10 000 N | 12 250 N |

An engine is applying 10 000 N to a train in a forwards direction.

The motion is being opposed by friction of 750 N and air resistance of 1500 N.

The resultant force acting on the train is ....

9 Electricity P1 • Grade 4–5

Complete the sentence.

Choose the answer from the box.   [1 mark]

| resistance of | power rating of | energy transferred by | voltage of |

Divide the potential difference across a lamp by the current flowing through it to find out

the .... the lamp.

10 Energy P1 • Grade 4–5

This question is about energy stores.

Complete the sentence.

Choose the answer from the box.   [1 mark]

| gravitational potential | chemical | kinetic | strain potential |

A toy car rolls down a ramp and off across the floor.

When it reaches the bottom of the ramp, its .... energy store is at its highest level for the whole journey.

Total score: .... / 24

Give

Only a short answer is required, not an explanation or a description.

Example question

1 **Bonding, Structure, and the Properties of Matter P1 • Grade 4–5**

Fullerenes are molecules of carbon atoms with hollow shapes.

a)   Give the name of the first fullerene that was discovered.   **[1 mark]**

b)   Give **one** use of this fullerene.   **[1 mark]**

Complete the example

2 Organisation P1 • Grade 1–3

The human heart has four chambers. There are blood vessels that either carry blood into these chambers or allow blood to leave the heart.

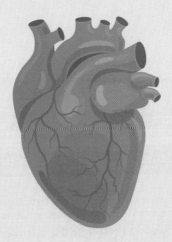

a) Give the name of the type of blood vessel that carries blood away
   from the heart.   [1 mark]

   Artery

b) Give the name of the chamber that pumps blood out to the lungs.   [1 mark]

c) Give the name of the blood vessel that returns blood to the heart
   from the lungs.   [1 mark]

3 Energy P1 • Grade 4–5 😊

Some students are determining the spring constant of a spring by hanging loads on it and taking measurements.

Give **two** precautions they should take when carrying out this experiment to minimise the risk of an accident.   [2 marks]

> There are more than two possible answers, however the points are separate and distinct, which is important.

1 The base of the stand should be _____ so that it can't

   _____.

2 The total weight should be _____ so that _____

   _____.

Exam practice questions

1   Homeostasis and Response ⓟ2 • Grade 1–3

It is important to keep the blood glucose concentration within narrow limits.

a) Give the name of a hormone that is produced to control the blood glucose concentration. [1 mark]

b) Give the name of the organ that produces this hormone. [1 mark]

2   Organic Chemistry ⓟ2 / Chemistry of the Atmosphere ⓟ2 • Grade 1–3

Coal is a fossil fuel that is burned to provide heat in our homes.

a) Give the name of the gas used in the combustion of coal. [1 mark]

b) Give the name of the greenhouse gas that is made when coal is used. [1 mark]

c) Sulfur impurities can be found in coal that release acidic gases when it is used.

Give the name of pollution that this causes. [1 mark]

3   Electricity ⓟ1 • Grade 1–3 🔒

A student is provided with an assortment of different pieces of wire and measures the resistance of each of them.

Give **three** factors that affect the resistance of a piece of wire. [3 marks]

1

2

3

4   Infection and Response ⓟ1 • Grade 4–5

Vaccinations can provide immunity.

Give **one** other way by which a person can become immune to a pathogen. [1 mark]

5 Organisation ⓟ • Grade 4–5

Read the passage about different types of cancer.

> Cancer can cause tumours to form in the body.
>
> There are two types of tumours caused by cancer. Benign tumours are contained in one area but another type of tumour can spread.
>
> Various lifestyle factors, such as sunbathing, can act as risk factors for cancer.

Answer these questions about the passage.

a) Give the name of the type of tumour that can spread.   **[1 mark]**

....

b) Give a risk factor for cancer that is **not** a lifestyle factor.   **[1 mark]**

....

6 Inheritance, Variation and Evolution ⓟ • Grade 4–5

The picture shows a fossil.

Many fossils are of animals that are extinct.

a) Give **three** factors that could contribute to the extinction of a species.   **[3 marks]**

1 ....

2 ....

3 ....

b) Give an example of a species that is now extinct.   **[1 mark]**

....

7 Inheritance, Variation and Evolution ⓟ2 • Grade 4–5

The figure shows layers of rock in a cliff.

Fossils were found of two different fish (**A** and **B**) in two different layers of rock.

One fossil was of a vertebrate fish. These fish first appeared in the fossil record about 450 million years ago.

The second fossil was of an Ostracoderm, a type of jawless fish. These jawless fish lived 530 million years ago.

a) Give the letter that represents the Ostracoderm. **[1 mark]**

....

b) Give a reason for your answer. **[2 marks]**

....

....

8 Energy ⓟ1 • Grade 4–5

Oil is described as a non-renewable energy resource.

Give **two** other non-renewable energy resources. **[2 marks]**

1 ....

2 ....

9 Organic Chemistry P2 • Grade 4–5

Methane, CH_4, is an alkane.

Alkanes are saturated hydrocarbons.

a) Give the general formula for alkanes. [1 mark]

....

b) Give the formula for the fourth member of the alkane homologous series. [1 mark]

....

10 Atomic Structure and the Periodic Table P1 • Grade 4–5

An isotope of sodium can be represented by the symbol $^{24}_{11}Na$.

Give the number of each subatomic particle in this atom of sodium. [2 marks]

Protons: ....

Neutrons: ....

Electrons: ....

11 Atomic Structure and the Periodic Table P1 • Grade 4–5

The elements in Group 7 and Group 1 can react together to make ionic compounds.

Group 1 metals are all examples of alkali metals.

a) Give the name used to describe all elements in Group 7. [1 mark]

....

b) Group 7 elements make molecules consisting of two atoms.

Give the formula of a molecule of chlorine. [1 mark]

....

c) Give the formula of the ions formed when potassium and bromine react to form an ionic compound. [2 marks]

....

....

12 Particle Model of Matter P1 • Grade 4–5

A student is determining the density of the rectangular solid block shown.

They have been provided with the block, a ruler and a weighing balance.

Give **four** measurements they will need to take to enable them to calculate the density. **[4 marks]**

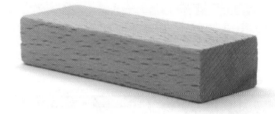

1 ....

2 ....

3 ....

4 ....

13 Forces P2 • Grade 4–5

A driver is driving a car along a road at speed.

A van comes out of a side road and the car driver reacts by applying the brakes and slowing down.

a) Give **three** factors which may affect the thinking distance the car travels.   **[3 marks]**

1 ....

2 ....

3 ....

b) Give **three** factors which may affect the braking distance the car travels.   **[3 marks]**

1 ....

2 ....

3 ....

14 Forces ② • Grade 4–5 🔄

The diagram shows a set of apparatus that is set up to investigate the acceleration of a vehicle along a horizontal air track.

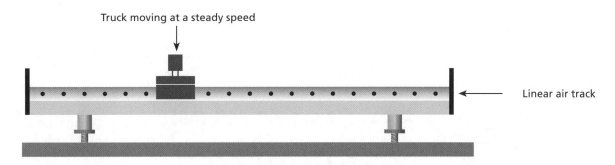

Truck moving at a steady speed

Linear air track

Air is being blown up through the track to support the vehicle.

Give **three** factors that will affect the acceleration of the vehicle.   [3 marks]

1 ....

2 ....

3 ....

15 Energy ① • Grade 4–5

The table shows the main sources of energy used for electricity generation in Britain in 2015.

Source of energy	Amount (%)
Coal	28.2
Oil and other	2.6
Gas	30.2
Nuclear	22.2
Renewables	16.7

a) Hydroelectricity is a renewable source.

Give **two** other renewable energy sources.   [2 marks]

1 ....

2 ....

b) Give **one** advantage and **one** disadvantage of nuclear power.   [2 marks]

....

....

Total score: .... / 45

Identify

Decide which is the correct name or characteristic from a list.

Worked example and more!

TOP TIP
You will usually be given some information or data to allow you to make your choice.

Example question

1 **Cell Biology P1 • Grade 1–3**

The table gives information about the features of three different cells, X, Y and Z.

Cell	Feature		
	Cell wall	Plasmids	Nucleus
X	present	present	absent
Y	present	absent	present
Z	absent	absent	present

a)   Identify which cell, X, Y or Z, could be an animal cell.   **[1 mark]**

b)   Identify which cell, X, Y or Z, is prokaryotic.   **[1 mark]**

c)   Identify which cells, X, Y or Z, contain mitochondria.   **[1 mark]**

Complete the example

2 Atomic Structure and the Periodic Table ⓟ • Grade 1–3

The figure below shows part of the Periodic Table. The symbols of the elements have been replaced with letters.

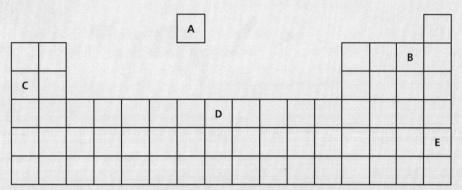

a)   Identify an element that has one electron in the outer shell.   C................................. **[1 mark]**

b)   Identify an element that has a full outer shell of electrons.   .... **[1 mark]**

3 Atomic Structure ⓟ • Grade 4–5

This diagram summarises information about different types of radioactive emissions and their ability to penetrate various materials.

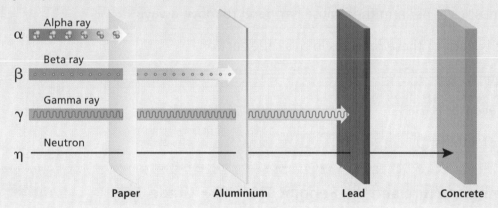

a)   Identify which type of radiation cannot penetrate paper.   **[1 mark]**

   Alpha

b)   Identify which type of material can prevent both alpha and beta radiation but not gamma rays or neutrons.   **[1 mark]**

   Aluminium

c)   Identify which type of radiation can penetrate aluminium but not lead.   **[1 mark]**

d)   Identify which material will prevent the passage of gamma rays but not neutrons.   **[1 mark]**

Exam practice questions

1 Ecology P2 • Grade 1–3

The diagram shows a food chain.

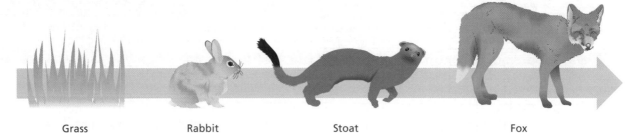

Grass   Rabbit   Stoat   Fox

a) Identify the producer. **[1 mark]**

....

b) Identify the secondary consumer. **[1 mark]**

....

2 Homeostasis and Response P2 • Grade 1–3

Jane touches a hot plate which stimulates nerve endings in her fingers.

Nerve impulses reach her spinal cord and then pass to muscles in her arm.

The muscles in her arm then cause her hand to move away.

Identify each of these features in this reflex action. **[3 marks]**

The stimulus is ....

The receptor is ....

The effector is ....

3 Atomic Structure and the Periodic Table P1 • Grade 1–3

The figure shows the structure of a helium atom.

a) Identify the protons, neutrons and electrons. **[3 marks]**

A = ...

B = ...

C = ...

b) Identify the charge carried by a proton. **[1 mark]**

....

4 Energy P1 • Grade 1–3 🔒

The picture shows equipment set up to determine the specific heat capacity of water.

Water is placed in the cup and heated using the electrical heater, which has a known power rating.

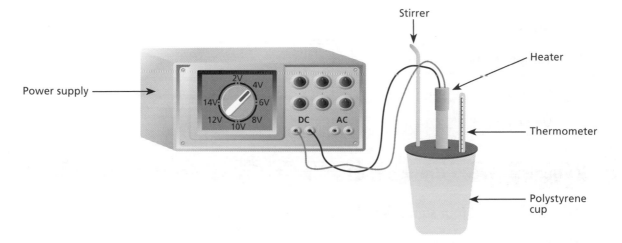

a) Identify how the temperature of the water is measured. **[1 mark]**

....

b) Identify how the energy transferred from the water to the surroundings is reduced. **[1 mark]**

....

c) Identify how the experimenter can ensure that all of the water is at a similar temperature. **[1 mark]**

....

5 Energy P1 • Grade 1–3

This list shows a number of different ways of generating electricity to power a home.

Identify the **three** methods that are renewable.

> **A** Gas turbine
>
> **B** Wind power
>
> **C** Oil fired
>
> **D** Nuclear
>
> **E** Tidal power
>
> **F** Hydro-electric power **[3 marks]**

1 ....

2 ....

3 ....

6 Energy ⓟ1 / Forces ⓟ2 • Grade 1–3

Identify which **two** of these factors will affect the amount of energy in the kinetic energy store of a moving object. Tick (✔) the **two** correct options. **[2 marks]**

Mass ☐

Temperature ☐

Height above ground ☐

Velocity ☐

7 Organisation ⓟ1 • Grade 4–5 🔒

A student tested four samples of food for different biological molecules.

The table shows the tests used and the results of the tests.

Food sample	Colour produced when the foods were tested		
	Test with iodine solution	Test with Benedict's solution	Test with Biuret solution
A	black	blue	blue
B	brown	blue	purple
C	brown	blue	blue
D	brown	orange	blue

a) Identify which food sample contains starch. **[1 mark]**

....

b) Identify which food samples contain carbohydrates. **[2 marks]**

....

c) Identify which food sample may contain an enzyme. **[1 mark]**

....

8 · Chemical Changes ⓟ • Grade 4–5

The photo below shows a sparkler.

Iron metal is used in sparklers. The iron reacts with a gas in the air to make sparks of iron oxide.

a) Identify the gas that iron reacts with. **[1 mark]**

....

b) Identify the type of chemical reaction happening in a lighted sparkler. **[1 mark]**

....

9 Atomic Structure and the Periodic Table ⓟ • Grade 4–5

Sodium is in Group 1 of the periodic table.

Identify a property of sodium.

Tick (✔) **one** box. **[1 mark]**

It floats on water.

It is a liquid at room temperature.

It does not conduct electricity.

It is a very unreactive gas.

A student wanted to investigate how changes in concentration of hydrochloric acid affect the rates of reaction with sodium thiosulfate. The student used the equipment below.

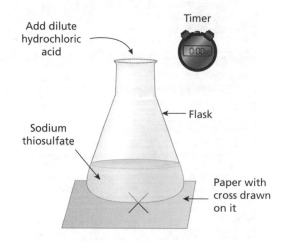

The student added the same volume of hydrochloric acid and sodium thiosulfate to a conical flask and timed how long it took until they could no longer see the cross.

a)   Identify the independent variable.   [1 mark]

....

b)   Identify the dependent variable.   [1 mark]

....

11 The Rate and Extent of Chemical Change P2 • Grade 4–5

A student wanted to investigate how adding a catalyst to hydrogen peroxide affected the rate of reaction.

The student used the equipment below.

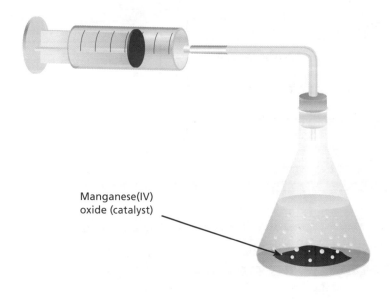

The student added hydrogen peroxide to a conical flask and recorded how much gas was collected every 10 seconds for two minutes.

The student did this experiment twice, once with a catalyst and once without.

a) Identify the dependent variable. [1 mark]

....

b) Identify a control variable. [1 mark]

....

12 Forces ② • Grade 4–5

This trolley is rolling down a ramp from the top to the bottom.

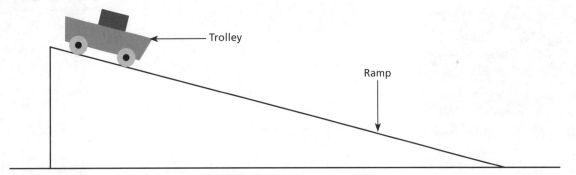

Identify, using the letters of the question, whereabouts on the ramp:

a) its velocity will be the greatest. [1 mark]

b) its kinetic energy will be the greatest. [1 mark]

c) its gravitational potential energy will be the greatest. [1 mark]

Total score: .... / 31

Name

Only a short answer is required, not an explanation or a description.

Worked example and more!

TOP TIP
A 'Name' question can often be answered with a single word, phrase or sentence.

Example question

1 Electricity **P1** • Grade 1–3

Name the piece of equipment that is used to measure the potential difference across a component in a circuit.

[1 mark]

Example question

2 Cell Biology P1 • Grade 1–3

The diagram shows six types of specialised cells from plants and animals.

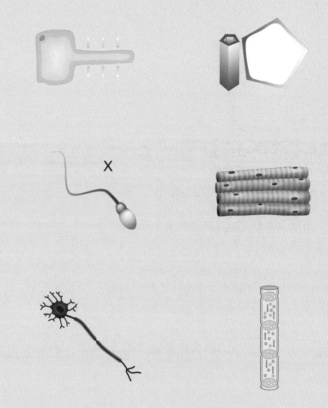

a)   Name the cell labelled X.   [1 mark]

<u>Sperm cell</u>

b)   Name the cell shown that has a cell wall thickened with lignin.   [1 mark]

c)   Name the cell shown that transports sugar around a plant.   [1 mark]

3 Atomic Structure and the Periodic Table P1 • Grade 1–3

This question is about compounds.

a)   Name the compound made when sodium reacts with chlorine.   [1 mark]

<u>Sodium</u>

b)   Name the elements in the compound lithium bromide.   [2 marks]

<u>Lithium and</u>

Exam practice questions

$\overset{\textcircled{\tiny }}{30}$

1 Organisation P1 • Grade 1–3

Blood is made of a number of different components.

a) Name the component that causes blood to clot. **[1 mark]**

....

b) Name the component that engulfs pathogens. **[1 mark]**

....

2 Atomic Structure and the Periodic Table P1 • Grade 1–3

This question is about the model of the atom.

a) Name the subatomic particle that has a 1+ charge. **[1 mark]**

....

b) Name the subatomic particle discovered by James Chadwick. **[1 mark]**

....

c) Name the scientist who suggested that electrons orbited the nucleus at specific distances. **[1 mark]**

....

3 Organic Chemistry P2 • Grade 1–3

Name the type of bonds found in alkane molecules.

Tick (✔) the correct box. **[1 mark]**

Metallic ☐

Ionic ☐

Single covalent ☐

Double covalent ☐

4 Energy P1 • Grade 1–3

Electricity is generated in power stations.

a) Name a fossil fuel that is used to generate electricity. **[1 mark]**

....

b) Name a renewable energy resource. **[1 mark]**

....

5 Electricity P1 • Grade 1–3

Name the circuit device represented by this symbol.

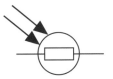

[1 mark]

....

6 Magnetism and Electromagnetism P2 • Grade 1–3

Name the type of electromagnetic radiation which has a wavelength longer than that of visible light but shorter than that of microwaves. [1 mark]

....

7 Forces P2 • Grade 1–3

Name the unit that is used to measure force. [1 mark]

....

8 Particle Model of Matter P1 • Grade 1–3

Name the device that is used in a laboratory to measure ionising radiation. [1 mark]

....

9 Infection and Response P1 • Grade 4–5

Pathogens may be viruses, bacteria, protists or fungi.

Name the type of pathogen that causes each of these diseases. [3 marks]

Rose black spot ....

Malaria ....

Measles ....

10 | Infection and Response P1 • Grade 4–5

Many drugs have been extracted from plants or microorganisms.

a)   Name the drug that has been extracted from foxgloves.   [1 mark]

....

b)   Name the plant that is used to extract aspirin.   [1 mark]

....

c)   Name the scientist who discovered penicillin.   [1 mark]

....

11 | Homeostasis and Response P2 • Grade 4–5

a)   Name the gland that releases follicle stimulating hormone (FSH).   [1 mark]

....

b)   Name the **three** hormones, which, along with FSH, control the menstrual cycle.   [3 marks]

1   ....

2   ....

3   ....

12 | Chemical Changes P1 • Grade 4–5

Lead bromide is an ionic compound. It can be separated by electrolysis.

a)   Name the element formed at the positive electrode during the electrolysis of
     molten lead bromide.   [1 mark]

....

b)   Name the element formed at the negative electrode during the electrolysis of
     molten lead bromide.   [1 mark]

....

13 Organic Chemistry P2 / Chemistry of the Atmosphere P2 • Grade 4–5

Natural gas is a fossil fuel and is used in our homes for heating and cooking.

Natural gas is mainly made of an alkane with one carbon atom.

a) Name the main hydrocarbon found in natural gas. [1 mark]

b) Name the chemical reaction for when natural gas is used to cook your food. [1 mark]

c) Name the greenhouse gas that is made when natural gas is used. [1 mark]

14 Chemistry of the Atmosphere P2 • Grade 4–5

Many scientists believe that human activities are causing the mean global temperature of the Earth to increase. They think this is due to an increase in the amounts of greenhouse gases in the atmosphere.

Water vapour is an example of a greenhouse gas.

Name **two** other greenhouse gases. [2 marks]

1

2

15 Atomic Structure and the Periodic Table P1 • Grade 4–5

Early models of atoms showed them as tiny spheres that could not be divided into simpler substances.

In 1897, Thomson discovered that atoms contained small, negatively charged particles. He proposed a new model, shown below.

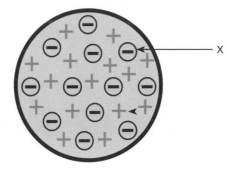

Name the particle labelled X. [1 mark]

Total score: .... / 30

Write

Recall a fact, definition or equation and write it down. Only a short answer is required, not an explanation or a description.

Worked example and more!

TOP TIP
The space provided will give an indication of the amount of detail needed.

Example question

1 **Forces P2 • Grade 4–5**

Write down the equation that connects acceleration, force and mass. **[1 mark]**

Complete the example

2 Bioenergetics P1 • Grade 1–3

Anaerobic respiration in yeast cells is used to manufacture useful products.

a) Write the word equation for anaerobic respiration in yeast cells. **[1 mark]**

Glucose →

b) Write **one** food and **one** drink that are made from fermentation using yeast. **[2 marks]**

3 Atomic Structure and the Periodic Table P1 • Grade 1–3

This question is about displacement reactions of halogens.

Chlorine water was mixed with a solution of potassium bromide.

A chemical reaction happened.

Potassium chloride and bromine were made.

Write a word equation for this reaction. **[2 marks]**

chlorine +   →   +

Exam practice questions

23

1 Inheritance, Variation and Evolution P2 • Grade 1–3

The table shows the common names and Latin names of some different cats.

Common Name	Latin Name
Bobcat	*Felis rufus*
Cheetah	*Acinonyx jubatus*
Ocelot	*Felis pardalis*
Lion	*Panthera leo*

Two of the cats are more closely related than the others.

Write down the common names of these two cats. **[2 marks]**

2 Bioenergetics ⓟ • Grade 1–3

During photosynthesis carbon dioxide and water react to produce glucose and oxygen.

Write a word equation for this reaction. **[1 mark]**

_____

3 Atomic Structure and the Periodic Table ⓟ • Grade 1–3

Sodium is a Group 1 metal that is stored under oil.

The figure below is a photograph of sodium metal in storage.

When sodium metal is removed from the oil it reacts with oxygen in the air. A white solid of sodium oxide is made.

Write a word equation for this reaction. **[2 marks]**

_____

_____

4 Chemistry of the Atmosphere ⓟ • Grade 1–3

Carbon dioxide is a greenhouse gas.

Write down the chemical formula of carbon dioxide. **[1 mark]**

_____

5 Electricity ⓟ • Grade 1–3 🔒

A student is testing a variety of materials to see which are electrical conductors.

Write down **three** pieces of equipment they will need to test the materials. **[3 marks]**

1 _____

2 _____

3 _____

6 Ecology P2 • Grade 4–5

Organisms in food webs can be named according to their trophic level.

a) Write the name given to herbivores that feeds on producers. **[1 mark]**

....

b) Write the name given to carnivores that do not have any predators. **[1 mark]**

....

c) Write the name given to carnivores that feed on herbivores. **[1 mark]**

....

7 Inheritance, Variation and Evolution P2 • Grade 4–5

Tom and Jake are identical twins. This means they have inherited the same genes from their parents.

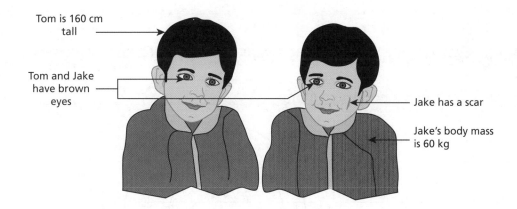

Tom is 160 cm tall

Tom and Jake have brown eyes

Jake has a scar

Jake's body mass is 60 kg

Write each of the characteristics from the image in the correct column of the table. **[4 marks]**

Controlled by their genes	Caused by the environment	Controlled by their genes and caused by the environment

Organic Chemistry P2 • Grade 4–5

Methane is the main hydrocarbon found in natural gas.

Natural gas is used for cooking and is combusted in gas boilers in homes to provide heat.

Write a word equation for the complete combustion of methane. **[2 marks]**

Atomic Structure and the Periodic Table P1 • Grade 4–5

The diagram shows a potassium atom.

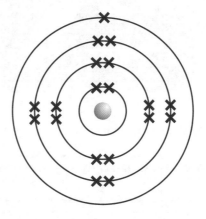

Write down the electron configuration of this potassium atom. **[1 mark]**

Energy P1 • Grade 4–5

Write down the equation used to calculate the gravitational potential energy of an object that has been raised up to a greater height. **[1 mark]**

11 Forces **P2** • Grade 4–5

A truck is travelling along a road at a steady speed.

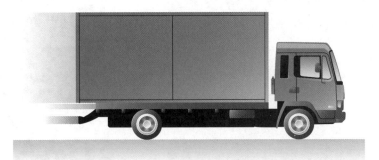

Write down the equation that can be used to calculate the speed of the truck.   **[1 mark]**

12 Energy **P1** • Grade 4–5

A solid material is at its melting point and is being melted.

Write down the **two** factors that will determine the amount of energy needed to melt it without raising its temperature.   **[2 marks]**

1 ....

2 ....

Total score: .... / 23

Complete

Write your answer in the space provided, for example on a diagram, in the gaps in a sentence or in a table.

Worked example and more!

TOP TIP
Fill in the gaps you know first. This can help narrow down the options for the remaining gaps.

Example question

1 **Atomic Structure and the Periodic Table P1 • Grade 1–3**

Complete the table about subatomic particles.   [3 marks]

Particle	Relative mass	Relative charge
Proton		1+
	1	0
Electron	0	

Complete the example

2 Ecology P2 • Grade 4–5

Peat bogs are dense wet areas of land that are acidic and low in nutrients.

The photograph shows an area of peat bogs in Scotland.

Complete these sentences about the destruction of peat bogs.   **[4 marks]**

Peat bogs are often destroyed to provide peat for .... *gardening* ....

The variety of different species that live there is called the .... and this is being reduced.

When the peat decays, it releases .... into the atmosphere. This can trap heat energy and cause

....

3 Electricity P1 • Grade 4–5

This diagram shows how electricity generated in a power station can be distributed to consumers using high voltage power lines.

Complete the diagram by adding the correct labels to the boxes.   **[4 marks]**

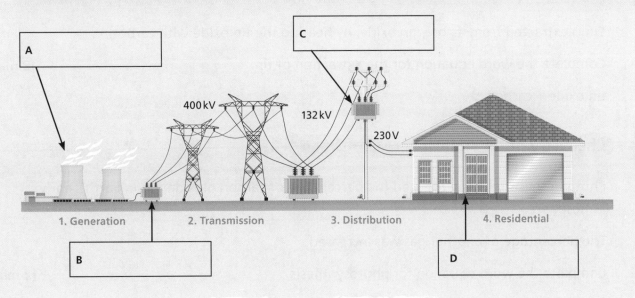

Exam practice questions

1 Ecology P2 • Grade 1–3

The diagram shows different stages in the water cycle.

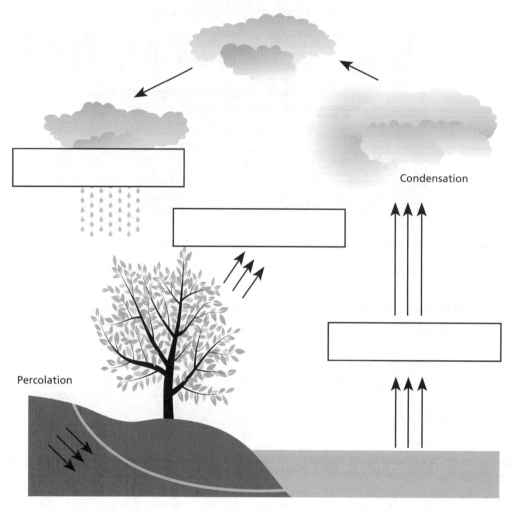

Condensation

Percolation

Complete the water cycle by writing in the names of the missing processes in the boxes.   **[3 marks]**

2 Chemical Changes P1 • Grade 1–3

Tin is extracted from its ore, tin oxide, by heating the tin oxide with carbon.

Complete the word equation for the extraction of tin.   **[2 marks]**

tin oxide + carbon → .... + ...

3 Chemistry of the Atmosphere P2 • Grade 1–3

Photosynthesis by algae reduced the percentage of carbon dioxide gas in Earth's early atmosphere.

The percentage of another gas was increased.

Complete the word equation for photosynthesis.   **[2 marks]**

.... + water → glucose + ...

4   Bonding, Structure, and the Properties of Matter ⓟ • Grade 1–3

Nitrogen and hydrogen form ammonia.

A hydrogen atom contains one electron.

A nitrogen atom contains five electrons in the outer shell.

Complete the dot-and-cross diagram for a molecule of ammonia.

Show the outer electrons only.   **[3 marks]**

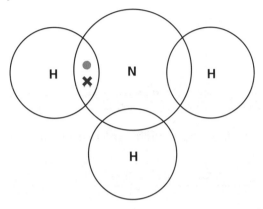

5   Particle Model of Matter ⓟ • Grade 1–3 🔒

This diagram shows apparatus set up to determine the volume of an irregularly shaped solid by immersing it in water.

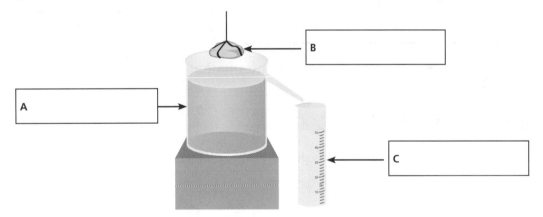

Complete the diagram by adding the labels to the apparatus.   **[3 marks]**

Measuring cylinder	Eureka can	Irregular solid

6 Inheritance, Variation and Evolution ② • Grade 4–5

Complete these sentences about the structure and function of the lungs.   **[4 marks]**

The lungs receive air from the mouth through a tube called the ....

This tube splits into two bronchi, which then divide into many smaller tubes called

....

These tubes end in air sacs called ....

The large number of air sacs increase the surface area of the lungs for

.... exchange.

7 Homeostasis and Response ② • Grade 4–5

The table shows some details about different human hormones.

Hormone	Site of production	Function
insulin	pancreas	....
testosterone	....	controls production of secondary sexual characteristics

Complete the table by giving the missing information.   **[2 marks]**

8 Organisation ① • Grade 4–5

The diagram shows a section through the human heart.

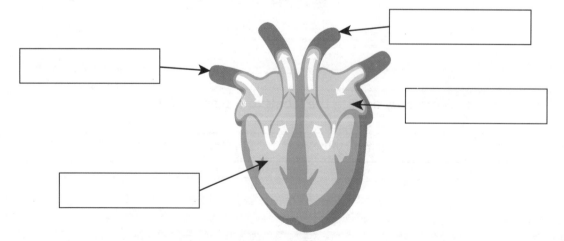

Complete the diagram by adding labels to the boxes.   **[4 marks]**

9 Cell Biology ⓟ • Grade 4–5 ⬤

In an osmosis experiment, potato cylinders are left in different concentrations of sugar solution.

The percentage change in mass of the cylinders is calculated.

The table shows the results of the experiment.

Concentration of sugar solution %	Percentage change in mass of cylinder
0	+10.1
0.2	+3.3
0.4	+1.2
0.6	−1.3
0.8	−4.5

Complete these sentences to explain the results of the experiment.   **[4 marks]**

The cylinder in 0% sugar solution .... in mass.

This is because .... entered the cell through a ....
permeable membrane.

The results show that the cytoplasm of the potato cells has a concentration approximately

equivalent to a .... % sugar solution.

10 Energy Changes ⓟ • Grade 4–5

This question is about energy changes.

Complete the sentences.   **[3 marks]**

An exothermic reaction is one that transfers energy to the ....

Endothermic reactions cause the temperature of the surroundings to ....

Hand warmers and self-heating cans are examples of everyday uses of ....

....

11

Bonding, Structure, and Properties of Matter ⓟ • Grade 4–5

Magnesium is a metal and can form a compound with oxygen.

A magnesium atom contains two electrons in the outer shell.

An oxygen atom contains six electrons in the outer shell.

Complete the dot-and-cross diagram for the compound of magnesium oxide. Show the outer electrons only. **[4 marks]**

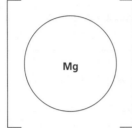 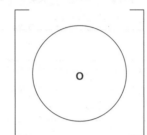

12

The Rate and Extent of Chemical Change ⓟ • Grade 4–5 ⊝

A student wanted to investigate the reaction between magnesium and hydrochloric acid.

The student used the equipment shown below.

The student investigated different concentrations of hydrochloric acid and measured the mass change to determine the rate of reaction with magnesium metal.

a) Complete the word equation for this reaction. **[2 marks]**

magnesium + hydrochloric acid → .... + ...

b) Complete the sentences. **[2 marks]**

The independent variable is ....

The dependent variable is ....

13 Chemical Analysis ② • Grade 4–5

A simple laboratory test for carbon dioxide is that limewater turns cloudy.

This is a chemical reaction where acidic carbon dioxide gas reacts with an alkali solution of calcium hydroxide.

A white precipitate of calcium carbonate is made.

Complete the balanced symbol equation by adding state symbols.   **[4 marks]**

CO_2 .... $+ Ca(OH)_2$ .... $\rightarrow CaCO_3$ .... $+ H_2O$ ....

14 Waves ② • Grade 4–5

The sentences are about various different electromagnetic waves and typical applications.

Complete the sentences by matching the uses with the types of radiation.

Gamma rays	Visible light	Ultraviolet	Radio waves
Infrared	X-rays	Microwaves	

a) .... enables objects to be seen by humans.

b)   Radio and TV signals use ....

c) .... is absorbed by skin and causes tan but can be dangerous in excess.

d) .... are used for cooking and also for communications.

e) .... produce images of inside the body.

f) .... transmits heat from hot objects.

g) .... are used as a medical treatment to kill cancerous cells but can also damage healthy cells.   **[7 marks]**

15 Energy ⓟ • Grade 4–5

The table shows various situations in which energy is being transferred.

Complete the table by filling in the gaps. **[3 marks]**

Situation	An energy store that is being filled	An energy store that is being depleted
Weight being dropped from a height.	Kinetic	a) ....
Climber reaching the top of a hill.	b)	Chemical
Spring being stretched by weights being hung on it.	c)	Kinetic

16 Energy ⓟ • Grade 4–5 🔳

The melting point of a type of wax is 80°C.

The graph shows how the temperature of a sample of the wax changes as it cools down and sets.

Complete the graph by adding the labels which show the state of the wax at each point. **[3 marks]**

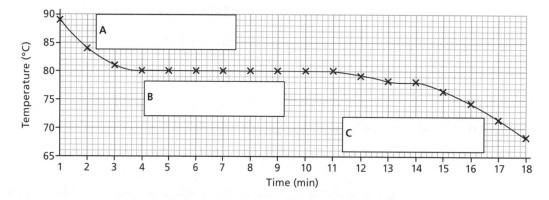

17 Energy ⓟ • Grade 4–5 🔒 🔳

The table shows the results for the stretching of a spring. Assume that the extension is directly proportional to the load throughout the range covered.

Load / N	0	10	20	30	A:	50	60
Extension / cm	0.0	3.5	7.0	B:	14.0	17.5	21.0

Complete the table by:

a) giving a value for load A.

b) giving a value for extension B. **[2 marks]**

The diagram shows a ripple tank set up to demonstrate wave behaviour.

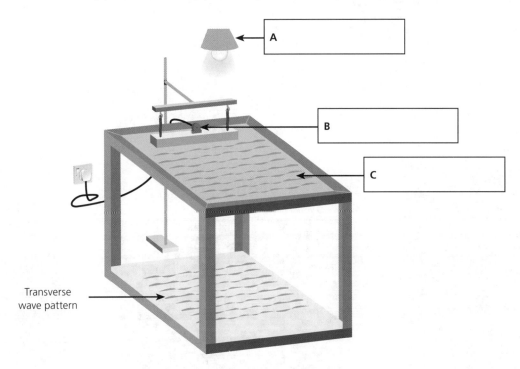

A

B

C

Transverse
wave pattern

Complete the diagram by labelling the equipment.

[3 marks]

Total score: / 60

Define

Give the exact meaning of a term or idea.

Worked example and more!

TOP TIP
Defining something means being very clear about what that thing is.

Example question

1 Inheritance, Variation and Evolution **P2** • Grade 1–3

The process of cloning organisms does not require fertilisation to occur.

a) Define the term **fertilisation**. [1 mark]

b) Define the term **cloning**. [2 marks]

Complete the example

2 Forces P2 • Grade 1–3

Define the term speed. [1 mark]

The rate

3 Chemical Analysis P2 • Grade 4–5

This question is about pure water.

In chemistry, distilled water is pure water but bottled spring water is not.

In everyday language, distilled water and mineral water are both examples of pure water.

a) Define **pure** in terms of chemistry. [1 mark]

A single

b) Define **pure** in terms of everyday language. [1 mark]

A substance that has had

Exam practice questions

⏱ 24

1 Cell Biology P1 • Grade 1–3

Plants take up water from the soil by the process of osmosis.

Define the term **osmosis**. [2 marks]

2 Chemistry of the Atmosphere $P2$ • Grade 1–3

The average carbon footprint in the UK is about 5000 kg CO_2e per person per year.

Define **carbon footprint**. [2 marks]

....

....

....

....

3 Organisation $P1$ • Grade 4–5

Transport in plants involves the processes of transpiration and translocation.

a) Define **transpiration**. [2 marks]

....

....

....

b) Define **translocation**. [2 marks]

....

....

....

4 Ecology $P2$ • Grade 4–5

In a pond ecosystem there is a varied community of organisms.

a) Define the term **ecosystem**. [1 mark]

....

....

b) Define the term **community**. [1 mark]

....

....

5   Energy Changes ⓟ • Grade 4–5

Hydrocarbon fuels undergo combustion reactions when they are used.

Usually a spark or flame will provide the activation energy to start the combustion reaction.

a)   Define **exothermic**.   **[2 marks]**

....

....

....

b)   Define **activation energy**.   **[1 mark]**

....

....

....

6   Chemistry of the Atmosphere ⓟ • Grade 4–5

In the UK, potable water is produced from an unpolluted source of fresh water.

Potable water contains low levels of dissolved substances.

Define **potable water**.   **[1 mark]**

....

7 Atomic Structure and the Periodic Table ⓟ • Grade 4–5

a) Define the term **atom**. [1 mark]

....

....

b) Define the term **ion**. [2 marks]

....

....

....

8 Waves ⓟ • Grade 4–5

Waves transfer energy between stores. Motion of a wave can be described by frequency.

Define the term **frequency**. [1 mark]

....

....

9 Energy ⓟ • Grade 4–5

Energy is always conserved but can be transferred between energy stores.

Define the term **kinetic energy**. [1 mark]

....

....

10 Energy ⓟ • Grade 4–5

Energy is always conserved but can be transferred between energy stores.

Define what is meant by **elastic potential energy**. [1 mark]

....

....

....

11 Energy ⓟ • Grade 4–5

Different substances need different amounts of energy to increase their temperature.

Define the term **specific heat capacity**. [1 mark]

....

....

....

12 Atomic Structure ⓟ • Grade 4–5

Some isotopes like carbon-13 are radioactive.

Define what is meant by the **half life of a radioactive isotope.** [1 mark]

....

....

....

13 Atomic Structure ⓟ • Grade 4–5

Radioactive isotopes can give out ionising radiation.

Define the term **radioactive contamination.** [1 mark]

....

....

14 Atomic Structure ⓟ • Grade 4–5

Foods are often irradiated to improve shelf life by reducing the number of microorganisms present.

Define the term **irradiation.** [1 mark]

....

....

Total score: .... / 24

Describe

You need to give the details of facts or processes in an organised way.

Worked example and more!

TOP TIP
In 'Describe' questions you are rewarded for giving a logical flow of information, so it can help to plan your answer as a bullet point list and think about the order you want to write the bullet points in.

Example question

1 Organisation **P1** • Grade 4–5

Describe the functions of bile in digestion. **[3 marks]**

Complete the example

The model of the atom has changed over time as new scientific evidence has been collected. In 1897, J.J. Thomson discovered the electron.

Describe the atomic model of the atom that J.J. Thomson proposed. **[2 marks]**

The atom is a ball of _____ charge with _____

_____ embedded in it.

This graph shows the motion of an object. **[4 marks]**

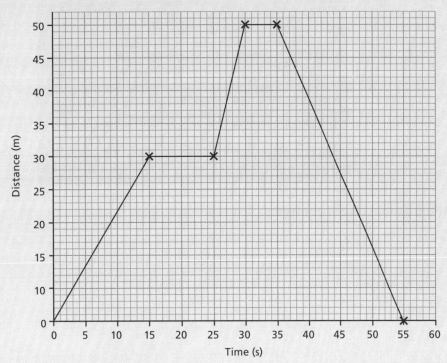

Describe the motion of the object.

The graph shows the relationship between distance and _____.

On a graph like this if the line is horizontal it means that the object is

_____. If the line has a positive gradient it means that the

object is _____.

In this graph the object starts off by travelling at a _____

and then _____. It then moves at a greater

_____ then

and finally _____

Exam practice questions

1 Organisation P1 • Grade 1–3

Describe how starch is digested in the human digestive system. [2 marks]

....

....

....

2 Organisation P1 • Grade 1–3

Smoking can be harmful to different systems in the human body.

Describe the possible harmful effects of smoking. [4 marks]

....

....

....

....

....

3 Bioenergetics P1 • Grade 1–3

This question is about separating mixtures.

Sand and water can be mixed together and separated by physical means.

Describe how to obtain a sample of pure dry sand from sandy water. [3 marks]

....

....

....

....

4   Chemical Analysis P2 • Grade 1–3 🏠

A student wanted to use chromatography to investigate a food colouring.

The figure below shows how the chromatogram was produced.

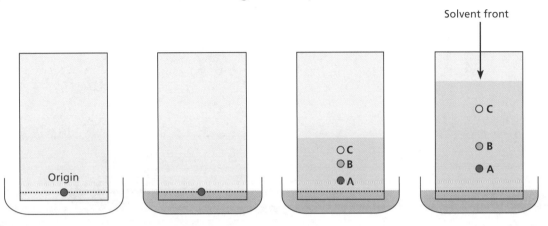

Describe what the chromatogram shows.   **[2 marks]**

....

....

5   Bonding, Structure, and the Properties of Matter P1 • Grade 1–3

The diagram shows how sodium and chlorine atoms form sodium chloride.

Only the outer electrons are shown.

The dots (•) and crosses (×) are used to represent electrons.

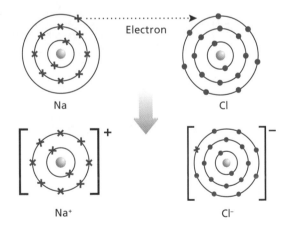

Describe, as fully as you can, what happens when sodium reacts with chlorine
to make sodium chloride.   **[4 marks]**

....

....

....

....

6 Inheritance, Variation and Evolution ⓟ • Grade 4–5

Fossils are the remains of organisms from millions of years ago.

Describe how fossils can be formed. **[4 marks]**

....

....

....

....

....

7 Bioenergetics ⓟ • Grade 4–5 ▤

The graph shows the results of an experiment to investigate the effects of percentage of oxygen in the air on the breathing rate.

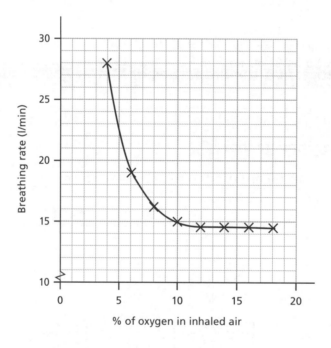

Describe the pattern of results shown by the graph.

Include data in your answer. **[3 marks]**

....

....

....

....

....

8   Ecology P2 • Grade 4–5 🔒

An ecologist wanted to determine the distribution and abundance of buttercup species in an ecosystem.

Describe how a quadrat can be used to measure the size of the buttercup population in an ecosystem. **[4 marks]**

....

....

....

....

....

....

....

9   Chemical Changes P1 / Chemical Analysis P2 • Grade 4–5 🔒

A student wanted to investigate the reaction between zinc metal and hydrochloric acid. The student placed a piece of zinc metal into a half-filled test tube of dilute hydrochloric acid.

a)   Describe the observations that the student would make. **[2 marks]**

....

....

....

b)   Describe a simple chemical test to show that one product of the reaction was hydrogen gas. **[2 marks]**

....

....

10   Atomic Structure and the Periodic Table P1 • Grade 4–5

This question is about the Periodic Table.

a)   Describe how elements were ordered before subatomic particles were discovered. **[1 mark]**

....

b) Describe how Mendeleev's Periodic Table was different to the earlier attempts to order elements. **[2 marks]**

....

....

....

c) Describe how the modern Periodic Table is different to Mendeleev's original. **[3 marks]**

....

....

....

11 Chemical Changes ⓟ / Chemical Analysis ⓟ • Grade 4–5 ⓐ

A student used electrolysis to investigate the products at the electrodes.

The student used the equipment shown in the diagram.

The gaseous products were collected.

In the investigation, samples of chlorine, hydrogen and oxygen gas were collected.

Describe how to test for each gas. **[6 marks]**

Chlorine: ....

....

Hydrogen: ....

....

Oxygen: ....

....

12

Atomic Structure and the Periodic Table ⓟ • Grade 4–5

An atom of Uranium decays to an atom of Thorium as represented by this equation:

$$^{233}_{92}U \rightarrow \, ^{229}_{90}Th + \, ^{4}_{2}He$$

Describe the difference between the Uranium and Thorium atoms in terms of protons and neutrons. **[2 marks]**

Protons:..

....

....

Neutrons:...

....

....

Electricity ⓟ • Grade 4–5

The diagram shows the internal wiring of a 13 A mains plug.

Describe **three** safety features of the plug, indicating how they keep the consumer safe. **[6 marks]**

1 ....

....

2 ....

....

3 ....

....

Waves ⓟ₂ • Grade 4–5

A slinky is a long, flexible coil of wire with a diameter of around 6–8 cm.

Describe how it can be used to represent both transverse and longitudinal waves. You may find it useful to include diagrams. **[4 marks]**

Transverse: ....

....

Longitudinal: ....

....

15 Magnetism and Electromagnetism P2 • Grade 4–5

The picture shows a solenoid.

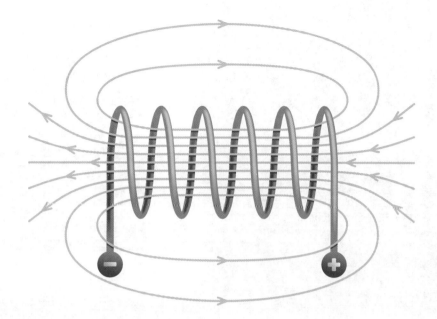

a) Describe the magnetic field inside the solenoid. **[2 marks]**

....

....

b) Describe the magnetic field outside the solenoid. **[1 mark]**

....

....

16 Electricity P1 • Grade 4–5

When a current flows through a metal, a magnetic field is produced.

Describe how the magnetic effect of a current can be demonstrated. **[4 marks]**

....

....

....

....

....

Total score: .... **/ 61**

Why/ What/ Which...

Why/What/Which/ Where/When/Who/How

These command words are used for direct questions to prompt short and precise answers.

Example question

1 | Cell Biology **P1** • Grade 4–5 🔒

Some students investigate the growth of onions.

They put an onion bulb in a jar of water. The bulb starts to grow roots.

Cells in the root tip are dividing.

Which part of the cell cycle involves cells dividing? **[1 mark]**

Complete the example

How is the extension of a spring calculated from its original length and its length with a load added? **[1 mark]**

Length when loaded

The diagram shows the difference in the structure between iron and steel.

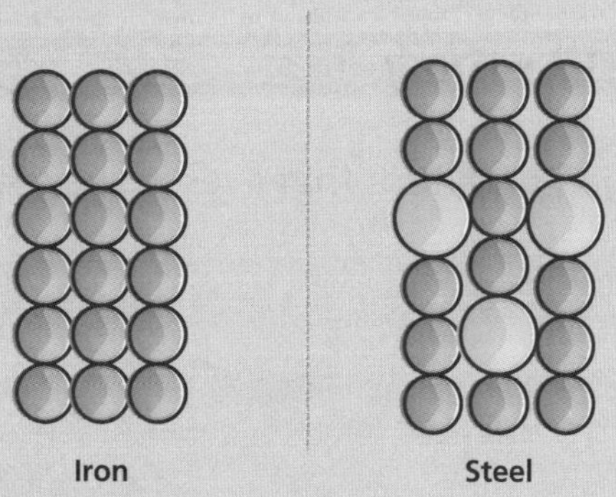

Iron   Steel

a) Which of the following words describe steel?

Tick (✓) **two** boxes. **[2 marks]**

> This is an AO2 question as you are asked to remember the definition of the key words and apply it to the example you are being given.
>
> Note that you are being asked to tick **two** boxes; there will be 1 mark for each correct answer.

Compound ☐

Mixture ☐

Element ☐

Formulation ☐

Aqueous solution ☐

b) Why are alloys harder than pure metals? **[2 marks]**

_In pure metals, the layers of _____ easily_

_over each other, but in alloys, the different sizes of _____

_distort the layers so they can't _____ as easily ._

Exam practice questions

1 Infection and Response P1 • Grade 1–3

Which drug acts as a painkiller?   [1 mark]

Tick (✔) **one** box.

aspirin ☐

digitalis ☐

penicillin ☐

2 Infection and Response P1 • Grade 1–3

Acetabularia is a single-celled organism that lives in the sea.

The diagram shows *Acetabularia*.

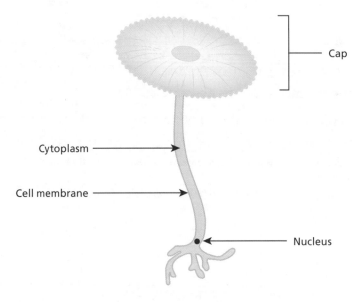

a) Which part of *Acetabularia* contains the genetic material?   [1 mark]

b) The genetic material is made up of long molecules.

What is the name of this molecule?

Tick (✔) **one** box.   [1 mark]

DNA ☐

fat ☐

protein ☐

sugar ☐

c) *Acetabularia* divides by mitosis. The list contains four steps in mitosis:

1. The cytoplasm and cell membranes divide.

2. The genetic material is doubled.

3. The nucleus divides.

4. One set of chromosomes is pulled to each end of the cell.

What is the order of these steps in mitosis? Write the numbers of the steps in the boxes in the correct order. **[3 marks]**

3 Using Resources ⓟ₂ • Grade 1–3

This question is about potable water.

In the UK, fresh water is filtered and sterilised to make potable water.

a) What is potable water?

Tick (✓) **one** box. **[1 mark]**

Rainwater ☐

Pure water ☐

Water that is safe to drink ☐

b) Which is a suitable sterilising agent to use for potable water?

Tick (✓) **one** box. **[1 mark]**

Oxygen ☐

Chlorine ☐

Carbon dioxide ☐

c) Why is potable water sterilised? **[2 marks]**

A student wanted to investigate the amount of energy released when metals react with acid.

This was the method used.

1. Measure 20 cm³ of hydrochloric acid into a polystyrene cup.

2. Measure the temperature of the hydrochloric acid.

3. Add 1 g of metal powder to the hydrochloric acid and stir.

4. Measure the highest temperature the mixture reaches.

5. Calculate the temperature increase for the reaction.

6. Repeat steps 1 to 5 with different metals.

a) What type of variable is the type of metal?

Tick (✓) **one** box. [1 mark]

Control ☐

Dependent ☐

Independent ☐

b) What type of variable is the mass of metal used?

Tick (✓) **one** box. [1 mark]

Control ☐

Dependent ☐

Independent ☐

c) What type of variable is the temperature?

Tick (✓) **one** box. [1 mark]

Control ☐

Dependent ☐

Independent ☐

5 Atomic Structure and the Periodic Table (P1) • Grade 1–3

This question is about subatomic particles.

a) Who provided evidence to show the existence of neutrons?

Tick (✓) **one** box.   **[1 mark]**

Bohr ☐

Chadwick ☐

Mendeleev ☐

b) Where in the atom are neutrons found?

Tick (✓) **one** box.   **[1 mark]**

In the nucleus of all atoms ☐

In the nucleus of most atoms ☐

In the atomic energy levels ☐

6 Atomic Structure (P1) • Grade 1–3

Which **two** types of ionising radiation consist of particles and not a wave?   **[2 marks]**

1 ....

2 ....

7 Inheritance, Variation and Evolution (P2) • Grade 4–5

What term describes all the genetic material found in an organism?   **[1 mark]**

....

8 Inheritance, Variation and Evolution (P2) • Grade 4–5

Cells can divide by meiosis.

Which of the following is a result of meiosis? Tick (✔) **one** box.   **[1 mark]**

Four genetically identical cells are produced. ☐

Four genetically different cells are produced. ☐

Two genetically identical cells are produced. ☐

Two genetically different cells are produced. ☐

9 Bioenergetics P1 • Grade 4–5

The diagram shows apparatus used to investigate the effect of carbon dioxide concentration on the rate of photosynthesis in pondweed.

The concentration of carbon dioxide is altered by adding different masses of sodium hydrogen carbonate to the beaker.

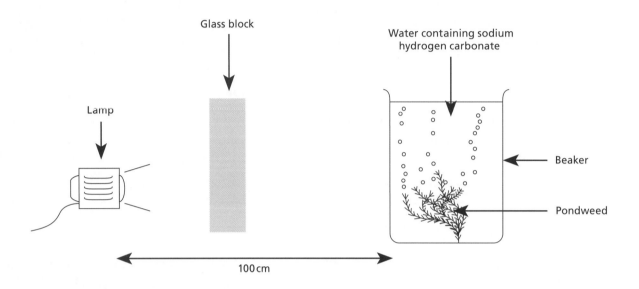

a) What is the function of the glass block in this experiment? **[1 mark]**

b) What is the dependent variable in this experiment? **[1 mark]**

10 Atomic Structure and the Periodic Table P1 • Grade 4–5

Chlorine has two stable isotopes.

The figure below shows the different symbols for each chlorine isotope.

$$^{35}_{17}Cl \qquad ^{37}_{17}Cl$$

Why is the mass number different for each isotope? **[1 mark]**

11 Forces P2 • Grade 4–5

What is the difference between speed and velocity? **[2 marks]**

12 Waves P2 • Grade 4–5

Why might central heating radiators in a building be more effective at radiating energy if they were painted matt black? **[2 marks]**

13 Atomic Structure P1 • Grade 4–5

Which type of ionising radiation has the greatest ability to ionise other particles it comes in contact with? **[1 mark]**

14 Forces P2 • Grade 4–5

Motion can be displayed on both distance–time graphs and on velocity–time graphs.

a) What does a horizontal straight line on a distance–time graph indicate about the motion of the object? **[1 mark]**

b) What does a horizontal straight line on a velocity–time graph indicate about the motion of an object? **[1 mark]**

Total score: .... / 29

Worked example and more!

Use

Base your answer on the information provided in the question.

TOP TIP
In some cases, you might be asked to use your own knowledge and understanding.

Example question

1 | **Bonding, Structure, and the Properties of Matter P1 • Grade 1–3**

Buckminsterfullerene is made of 60 carbon atoms that are held together by strong bonds. The figure below shows a molecule of Buckminsterfullerene.

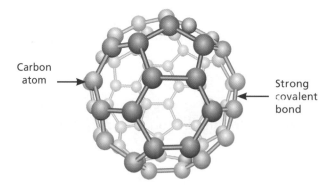

Carbon atom →

← Strong covalent bond

a)   What type of structure is Buckminsterfullerene? Tick (✔) **one** box.   **[1 mark]**

Use the figure to help you.

Lattice ☐   Molecule ☐   Giant covalent ☐

b)   Give the formula of Buckminsterfullerene.

Use the figure to help you.   **[2 marks]**

Complete the example

2 | Infection and Response ⓟ • Grade 4–5

Smallpox is a disease that killed millions of people. Due to vaccination, the disease has disappeared. The diagrams show how people were vaccinated for smallpox.

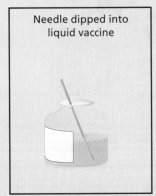
Needle dipped into liquid vaccine

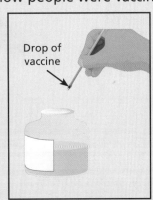
Drop of vaccine

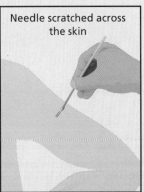
Needle scratched across the skin

Use the diagrams to suggest reasons why this method enabled large numbers of people to be vaccinated very quickly. **[2 marks]**

This method does not use .... equipment.

It is also very easy, so that people do not need a lot of ....

to be able to administer the vaccine.

3 | Energy ⓟ • Grade 4–5 🔢

The figure shows an energy transfer diagram for an LED light.

Electrical energy 4 Joules — Light 0.8 Joules — Thermal 3.2 Joules

Use the information provided on the diagram to work out:

a) The amount of energy transferred out of the light which is not useful. **[2 marks]**

The purpose is to produce .... so any other outputs are not

useful. The .... output is not useful and is ....

b) The efficiency of the light. **[2 marks]**

Efficiency = (Useful energy transferred out ÷ Total energy supplied) × 100

= .... ÷ .... × 100

= ....

1 Chemistry of the Atmosphere ② • Grade 1–3 ▦

The figure below shows the composition of dry air.

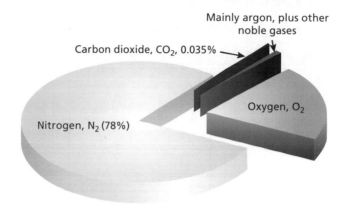

a) Name the element that mainly makes up dry air.

Use the figure above.   [1 mark]

....

b) Name the group of elements that make up about 1% of dry air.

Use the figure above.   [1 mark]

....

c) Give the approximate fraction of dry air which is made up of oxygen.

Use the figure above.   [1 mark]

....

2 Atomic Structure and the Periodic Table ① • Grade 1–3 ▦

This question is about halogens. The table shows the melting and boiling points of Group 7 elements.

Element	Melting point (°C)	Boiling point (°C)
Fluorine	−220	−188
Chlorine	−101	−35
Bromine	−7	59
Iodine	114	184

Room temperature is 25°C.

a) Name a halogen that is a gas at room temperature.   [1 mark]

Use the table above.

....

b) Describe the trend in melting point. [1 mark]

Use the table above.

....

....

c) Which halogen has the strongest intermolecular forces of attraction? [1 mark]

Use the table above. Tick (✓) **one** box.

Fluorine ☐

Chlorine ☐

Bromine ☐

Iodine ☐

3 Forces P2 • Grade 1–3 ▦

A piece of fruit has a mass of 0.2 kg.

gravitational field strength = 9.8 N/kg

Calculate the weight of the piece of fruit.

Use the equation:

weight = mass × gravitational field strength [2 marks]

....

....

....

4 Cell Biology P1 • Grade 4–5 ▦ ☺

A student took a swab of their own cheek cells.

The student measured the cells as 0.06 mm.

Calculate the image length if the cheek cell is viewed at x20 magnification.

Use the equation: $magnification = \dfrac{size\ of\ image}{size\ of\ real\ object}$ [3 marks]

....

....

....

Image length = ... mm

5 Infection and Response P1 • Grade 4–5

The diagram shows the life cycle of the pathogen that causes malaria.

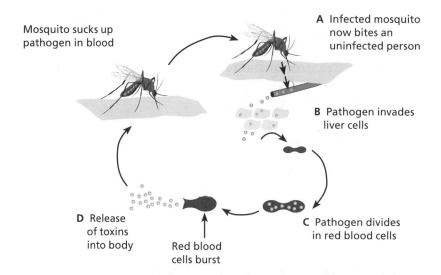

Mosquito sucks up pathogen in blood

A Infected mosquito now bites an uninfected person

B Pathogen invades liver cells

C Pathogen divides in red blood cells

D Release of toxins into body

Red blood cells burst

Use the information in the diagram to explain at which point, A, B, C or D, the person gets a fever. **[2 marks]**

6 Infection and Response P1 • Grade 4–5

Measles is a disease caused by a virus.

The graph shows the numbers of confirmed cases of measles in England and Wales.

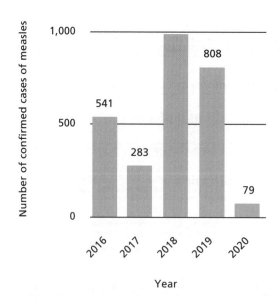

Use the graph to estimate the number of confirmed measles cases in England and Wales in 2018. **[1 mark]**

Atomic Structure and the Periodic Table ⓟ • Grade 4–5 🖩

The table gives some information about atoms.

Particle	Atom	Nucleus
Radius (m)	1×10^{-10}	1×10^{-14}

Name the smallest particle.

Use the table.

[1 mark]

Using Resources ⓟ • Grade 4–5 🖩

This question is about alloys.

a) High carbon steel is an alloy used in construction because it is strong.

The figure below shows a diagram of steel.

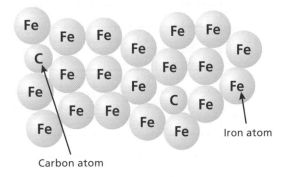

Carbon atom

Iron atom

Calculate the ratio of iron to carbon atoms in the sample of steel.

Use the figure above.

[2 marks]

b) Bronze is an alloy used to make church bells.

The figure below shows a diagram of bronze.

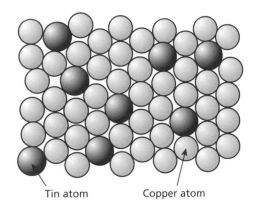

Tin atom   Copper atom

Calculate the percentage of copper atoms in the sample of bronze.

Give your answer to 3 significant figures.

Use the figure above. **[4 marks]**

....

....

....

....

9 Electricity ⓟ • Grade 4–5 ▦

Use the information in this table to plot a graph, showing the relationship between the potential difference across a diode and the current flowing through it. **[4 marks]**

Potential difference/V	Current/mA
0	0
0.5	0
1.0	0
1.5	0
2.0	1
2.5	2
3.0	3
3.5	4
4.0	5
4.5	6

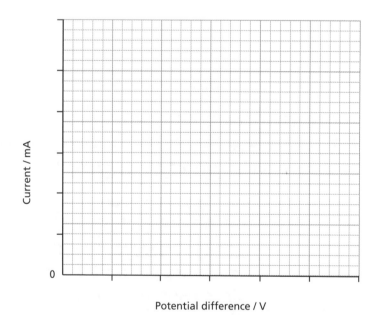

Current / mA

Potential difference / V

The picture shows an oscilloscope trace of a wave.

Each square on the oscilloscope is 1 second.

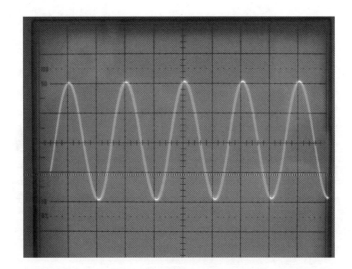

a) Use the image to determine the frequency of the wave. **[1 mark]**

Frequency = ... Hz

b) Calculate the period of this wave.

Use your answer to part a). If you have not got an answer to part a, then use a value of 10. **[3 marks]**

....

....

....

Period = ... s

Total score: .... / 29

Draw

Draw either a complete drawing or diagram, or add to one you are given.

Worked example and more!

TOP TIP
Artistic ability is not important, but clarity and accuracy are. Think about the key features you need to include and ensure that these can be understood.

Example question

1 **Electricity P1 / Magnetism and Electromagnetism P2 • Grade 1–3 😬**

A student is setting up an experiment to see how making a current flow through a coil of wire around a nail can produce a magnetic field.

Draw diagrams to show how:

a) the wire, nail and power supply should be set up   **[1 mark]**

b) the coil can then be tested to see whether it has a magnetic field.   **[1 mark]**

Complete the example

2 Cell Biology P1 • Grade 1–3

Different plant tissues perform specific functions.

Draw one line from each plant tissue to the function of the tissue. **[3 marks]**

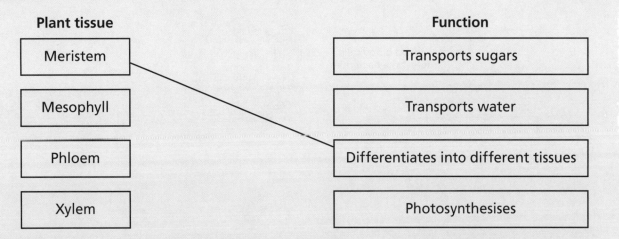

Plant tissue	Function
Meristem	Transports sugars
Mesophyll	Transports water
Phloem	Differentiates into different tissues
Xylem	Photosynthesises

3 Atomic Structure and the Periodic Table P1 • Grade 4–5

Magnesium is a Group 2 metal. Chlorine is a Group 7 non-metal.

Magnesium and chlorine can react together to make magnesium chloride.

Draw a dot-and-cross diagram to show what happens when atoms of magnesium and chlorine react to produce magnesium chloride. **[5 marks]**

When a metal and a non-metal react together, an ionic compound is formed.
Use square brackets to show each individual ion.
Remember that metals lose electrons and become positive ions. Non-metals gain electrons and become negative ions.

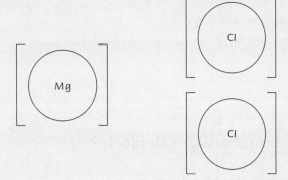

Exam practice questions

1 Infection and Response ⓟ₁ • Grade 1–3

White blood cells can destroy bacteria by phagocytosis.

Draw on this diagram the two missing steps in this process.

[2 marks]

White blood cells
detect the bacterium

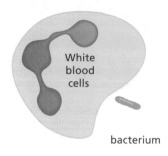

White
blood
cells

bacterium

Phagocytosis starts

Bacterium is engulfed

2 Chemistry of the Atmosphere ⓟ₂ • Grade 1–3

The combustion of fuels causes air pollution.

Draw **one** line from each gas to the environmental problem that it causes.

[2 marks]

Methane	Climate change
Sulfur dioxide	Global dimming
Particulates	Acid rain

3 Chemical Analysis ℗2 • Grade 1–3 😊

This question is about testing gases.

Draw **one** line from each gas to the test which shows it is present.   **[3 marks]**

Gas	Test
Hydrogen	Glowing splint relights
Carbon dioxide	Damp litmus paper turns white
Oxygen	Burning splint and hear a pop sound
Chlorine	Limewater turns milky

4 Electricity ℗1 • Grade 1–3 😊

Draw a circuit diagram to show how a battery, ammeter and voltmeter can be used to find the resistance of a wire.

You must use the correct circuit symbols.   **[3 marks]**

5 Cell Biology ⓟ • Grade 4–5 🏠

The photograph shows a cheek cell taken using a light microscope.

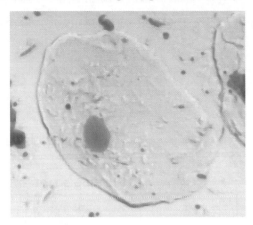

Draw a labelled biological drawing of the cheek cell.   **[3 marks]**

6 Atomic Structure and the Periodic Table ⓟ / Bonding, Structure, and the Properties of Matter ⓟ • Grade 4–5

Fluorine is a yellow gas at room temperature.

The proton number of fluorine is 9.

a) Draw the electronic structure of fluorine.   **[2 marks]**

b) Fluorine forms molecules at room temperature.

Draw a dot-and-cross diagram for a fluorine molecule.

Show only the outer shell electrons. **[2 marks]**

---

7 Electricity P1 • Grade 4–5

Draw a diagram with a cell and a lamp to show how:

a) a voltmeter should be connected to measure the potential difference across the lamp. **[1 mark]**

b) an ammeter should be connected to show the current flowing through the lamp. **[1 mark]**

---

8 Energy P1 • Grade 4–5

Some students are carrying out an experiment to measure the specific heat capacity of copper.

They have a thermometer, an electrical heater, a block of copper with holes to accommodate the thermometer and heater, wires, a power supply, ammeter and voltmeter.

Draw a diagram to show how this equipment should be set up to produce a set of readings that will enable the specific heat capacity to be calculated. **[4 marks]**

9 **Electricity P1 • Grade 4–5**

Some students are investigating the relationship between the length of a piece of copper wire and its resistance.

They have a ruler, copper wire, connecting wires, ammeter, voltmeter and power supply.

Draw a diagram showing how this equipment should be set up to produce data that will allow the resistance of a particular length of wire to be determined. **[4 marks]**

The figure shows a weather balloon filled with helium gas at a temperature of 0°C.

Draw a diagram to show the arrangement of helium atoms at 0°C.

Draw 10 circles to represent the helium atoms.   **[1 mark]**

Total score: _____ / 28

Sketch

Draw approximately: your drawing doesn't need to be accurate but you should include enough information to demonstrate your understanding of the principles.

Worked example and more!

TOP TIP
The difference between draw and sketch is that more accuracy is expected when drawing whereas sketching involves a degree of approximation.

Example question

1   **The Rate and Extent of Chemical Change ⓟ2 • Grade 4–5** 😊

Rusting is a chemical reaction.
The rate of reaction for the rusting of an iron nail can be monitored by measuring the mass change.

The graph shows the rate of reaction for the rusting of an iron nail.

On the graph, sketch the results you would expect if you used iron powder.   **[3 marks]**

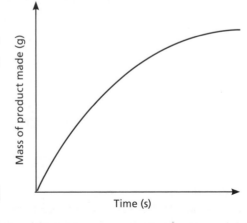

Complete the example

2 Forces ② • Grade 1–3 😣

A student investigated the current through an ohmic conductor.

The diagram shows the circuit that the student used.

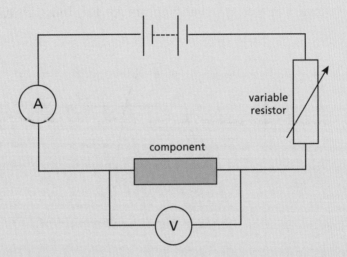

The student discovered that if the temperature remained constant, the resistance was constant as the current changed.

Sketch the graph of the student's results.   **[2 marks]**

In the rubric, the shape of the graph is explained: the graph is directly proportional and so it needs to be a straight line through the origin.

This means that resistance will be constant as the potential difference increases at the same rate as the current and allows the calculation of 'resistance = current × potential difference' to be correctly shown.

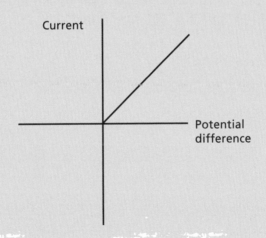

Exam practice questions

1 Energy Changes P1 / The Rate and Extent of Chemical Change P2 • Grade 4–5

Zinc can react with hydrochloric acid.

Copper powder can be used as a catalyst to increase the rate of reaction.

The figure below shows the energy level diagram for this reaction without a catalyst.

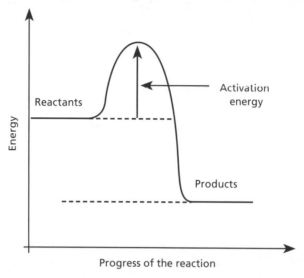

On the figure above, sketch the effect of adding a catalyst to this reaction. **[2 marks]**

2 The Rate and Extent of Chemical Change P2 • Grade 4–5

A student investigated the volume of gas produced when large lumps of calcium carbonate reacted with hydrochloric acid.

The figure below shows the results of the experiment.

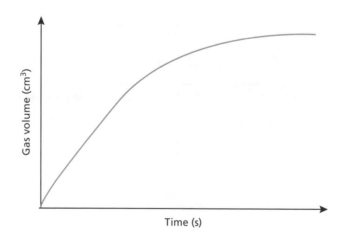

On the figure above, sketch the results you would expect if the student doubled the concentration of the acid. **[3 marks]**

3   Bonding, Structure, and the Properties of Matter ℗ • Grade 4–5

Sodium chloride (NaCl), is an example of an ionic compound.

Ionic compounds form a lattice made of a giant structure of ions.

Sketch the structure of sodium chloride. You must include at least 5 sodium ions and 5 chloride ions in your sketch.

[3 marks]

4   The Rate and Extent of Chemical Change ℗ • Grade 4–5

Hydrogen peroxide (H_2O_2) can decompose into oxygen (O_2) and water (H_2O).

Here is the reaction profile diagram for this reaction.

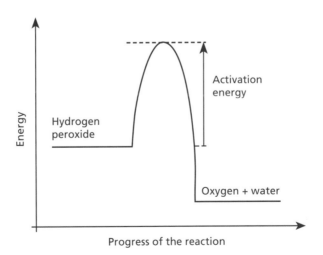

Manganese dioxide (MnO_2) can catalyse this reaction.

Sketch on the diagram the activation energy when manganese dioxide is added.   **[1 mark]**

5 **Energy** **P1** • **Grade 4–5**

Sketch a graph to show how the temperature of a substance will change if, over a period of time, it is cooling as a liquid, then freezing, and then cooling as a solid. **[3 marks]**

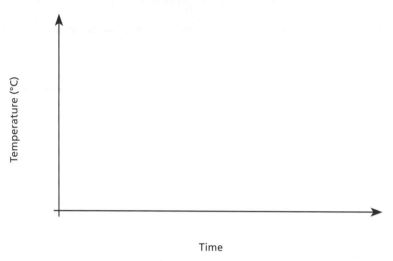

6 **Waves** **P2** • **Grade 4–5**

A ripple tank can be used to demonstrate waves. The diagram shows waves produced by a ripple tank.

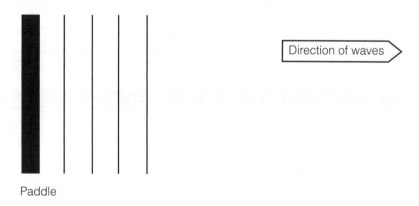

In 2 s the paddle moves up and down creating waves.

Sketch on the diagram what would be seen after a further 2 s. **[2 marks]**

7 Electricity ℗ • Grade 4–5

The resistance of a filament lamp changes as the temperature of the filament increases.

Sketch a current–potential difference graph for a filament lamp. **[2 marks]**

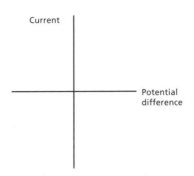

8 Electricity ℗ • Grade 4–5

A diode is an electrical component that allows current to flow in only one direction. Look at the picture and the conventional circuit diagram of a diode.

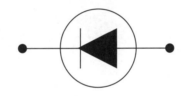

Sketch a current–potential difference graph for a diode. **[2 marks]**

Total score: .... / 17

Label

Add the appropriate names of structures or processes to a diagram.

Worked example and more!

TOP TIP
Make sure you add clear labels and, where required, clear arrows that show where the labels point.

Example question

1 **Electricity P1 • Grade 1–3** 😊

Label the circuit diagram.   [5 marks]

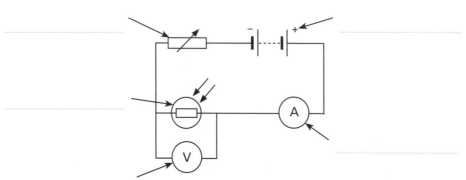

Complete the example

Potable water can be made from the distillation of sea water.

The figure below shows the equipment that can be used.

a) Label the piece of equipment that causes the evaporation of sea water. **[1 mark]**

> Evaporation uses energy so you need to think about which part of the diagram is a heating apparatus.
>
> Then label it as 'a)' or name the equipment.

b) Label the piece of equipment that causes condensation of the pure water. **[1 mark]**

> The steam needs to be cooled and condensed back to liquid water.
>
> Choose the apparatus in the diagram that is cooling and label it as 'b)' or name the equipment.

The diagram shows the main hormone-producing glands in the human male body.

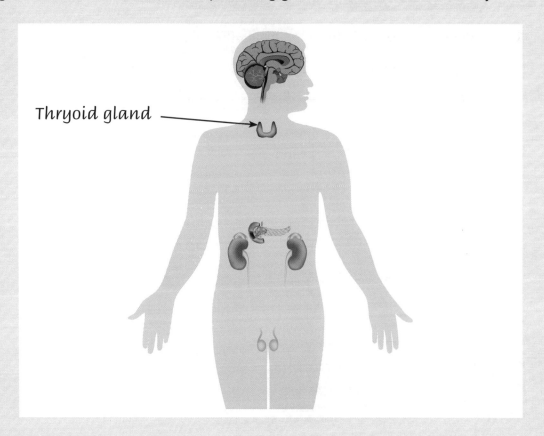

Thryoid gland

Label the diagram to show the position of:

- the thyroid gland

- the pituitary gland

- the pancreas

- an adrenal gland.

[4 marks]

Exam practice questions

1 Cell Biology P1 • Grade 1–3

The diagram shows a palisade mesophyll cell from a plant leaf.

Label the diagram to show the main structures of the cell. **[5 marks]**

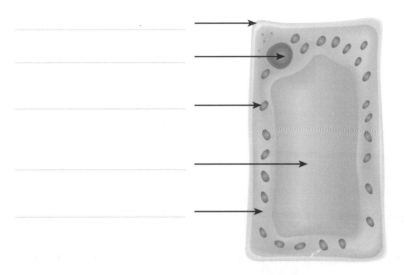

2 Atomic Structure and the Periodic Table P1 • Grade 1–3

The figure below is a representation of a sodium atom.

$$^{23}_{11}\text{Na}$$

Label the atomic number and the mass number on the figure. **[1 mark]**

3 Atomic Structure and the Periodic Table P1 • Grade 1–3

Beryllium is a metal element.

The figure below shows the atomic structure of beryllium, including the subatomic particles.

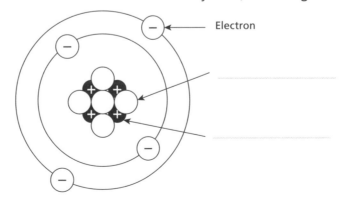

Electron

An electron is already labelled.

Label the subatomic particles that are found in the centre of the atom. **[2 marks]**

4 Electricity ℗ • Grade 1–3 😊

Label this circuit diagram to show what each of the symbols represents. **[3 marks]**

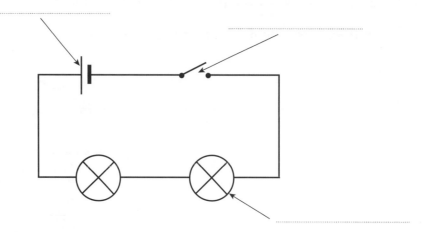

5 Energy ℗ • Grade 1–3 😊

This diagram shows equipment set up to determine the specific heat capacity of a metal.

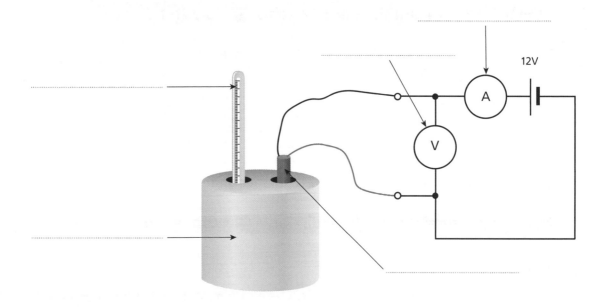

Label the diagram to show the:

- metal (being tested)
- thermometer
- ammeter
- voltmeter
- heater **[5 marks]**

6 Electricity ① • Grade 1–3 ☺

The diagrams show two circuits set up to compare the resistance of two resistors connected in series with the same two resistors connected in parallel.

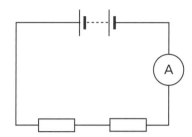 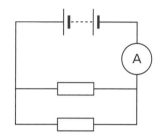

Label the diagrams to show the:

- resistors in series
- resistors in parallel
- ammeter
- battery.

[4 marks]

7 Forces ② • Grade 1–3 ☺

This diagram shows apparatus set up to explore the relationship between the force applied to a spring and its extension.

Label the diagram to show the:

- spring
- load added
- pointer used to measure length of spring.

[3 marks]

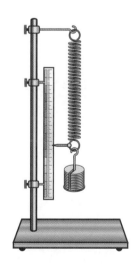

Organisation ⓟ • Grade 4–5

The diagram shows a section through a human heart.

Label the heart to show the position of:

• the natural pacemaker

• a valve that stops blood passing back into the right atrium from the right ventricle.

[2 marks]

Cell Biology ⓟ • Grade 4–5

The diagram shows details of cells at different stages of the cell cycle.

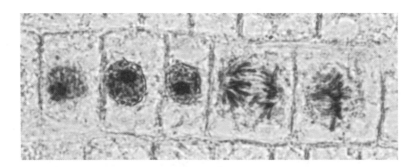

Label the diagram with the letters R, S and T to indicate the cell that is in each of these stages of the cell cycle:

R – a cell that is replicating its DNA and sub-cellular structures

S – a cell that is just starting mitosis

T – a cell that is about to divide

[3 marks]

Energy Changes ⓟ • Grade 4–5

The figure shows the energy level diagram for the combustion of methane.

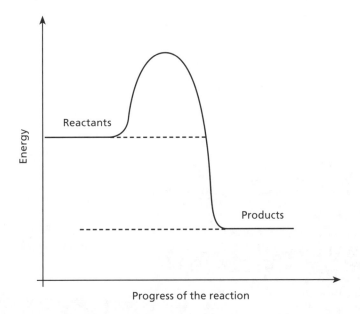

Reactants

Energy

Products

Progress of the reaction

a) Label the activation energy on the figure.   **[1 mark]**

b) Label the overall energy change on the figure.   **[1 mark]**

11

Energy Changes ⓟ • Grade 4–5

The reaction of citric acid and sodium hydrogencarbonate is endothermic.

The figure below shows the energy level diagram for the reaction of citric acid with sodium hydrogencarbonate.

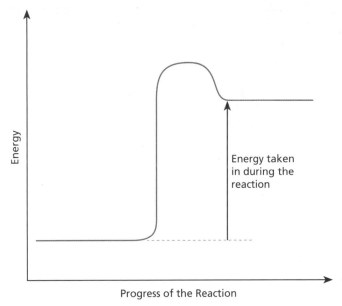

Energy

Energy taken
in during the
reaction

Progress of the Reaction

a) Label the reactants and products on the figure.   **[1 mark]**

b) Label the activation energy on the figure.   **[1 mark]**

Total score: .... **/ 32**

Suggest

Apply your knowledge and understanding to a given situation. Do not expect to have learnt the answer.

Worked example and more!

TOP TIP
The examiner wants to see an indication of what is likely to happen; your response needs to be plausible.

Example question

1 Using Resources **P2** • Grade 1–3

Sea water can be made into potable water by distillation.

Suggest why distilled water is safe to drink.   **[1 mark]**

Complete the example

2 Inheritance, Variation and Evolution ㉒ • Grade 4–5

Scientists have been investigating a large area of seagrass plants that are growing in the sea off the coast of Australia.

The area covers 200 sq km.

They have tested the DNA from a large number of plants.

They found that the DNA from all the plants was identical.

Suggest how the plants started growing in the area and produced enough plants to cover the entire area. **[3 marks]**

A plant may have sexually reproduced and released _____ .

These were carried to the area and germinated to produce a plant.

This plant must then have used _____ reproduction many

times as all the plants in the area are _____ identical.

3 Electricity ㉑ • Grade 4–5

A group of students set up a circuit with three lamps in series with a 4.5 V battery. The lamps are all marked 1.5 V 200 mA and they all light up when the circuit is completed.

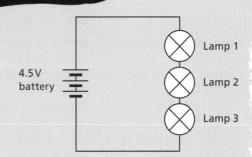

a) Suggest why one of the lamps is very slightly brighter than the others. **[2 marks]**

The lamps are the same design but may _____ slightly in

manufacture or have been treated _____ . This may result in one

of them having a slightly _____ resistance and therefore being

slightly _____ .

b) Suggest what will happen to the brightness of these lamps if a fourth lamp is now added in series with them. **[2 marks]**

If a fourth lamp is added, the potential difference will be _____

between four lamps instead of _____ . This means there will be less

_____ across each lamp and they will all be

_____ than before.

Exam practice questions

24

1   Inheritance, Variation and Evolution P2 • Grade 1–3

The diagram shows a potato plant that has grown from a potato tuber.

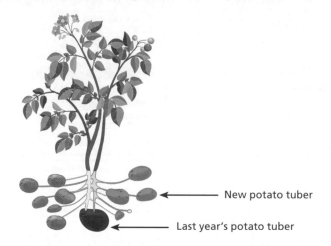

← New potato tuber

← Last year's potato tuber

a) Suggest how this potato plant can make several genetically identical plants next year. **[2 marks]**

....

....

....

b) There are thousands of different varieties of potato growing in the world.

Most of these have been produced by selective breeding.

Suggest **two** features that might be selected for in potato plants. **[2 marks]**

1 ....

2 ....

2   Using Resources P2 • Grade 1–3

Rings are a type of jewellery and often made of metal.

The picture shows two rings.

a) Suggest **one** reason why pure gold is rarely used for jewellery. **[1 mark]**

....

b) Suggest **one** way that gold is usually used in jewellery.

[1 mark]

....

3 **Energy ⓟ • Grade 1–3**

This house has solar panels on the roof.

The solar panels use sunlight to generate electricity and this has reduced the electricity bill of the household.

Suggest why the homeowner fitted solar panels and a battery rather than just solar panels.

[2 marks]

....

....

....

....

4 **Energy ⓟ • Grade 1–3 🏠**

A student is heating a beaker of water.

There is a thermometer in the water so that the temperature can be monitored.

After a few minutes they remove the thermometer from the water to read it.

Suggest why this will not give an accurate value for the temperature of the water.   [1 mark]

....

....

....

5 Organisation P1 • Grade 4–5

The diagram shows a food web in the sea.

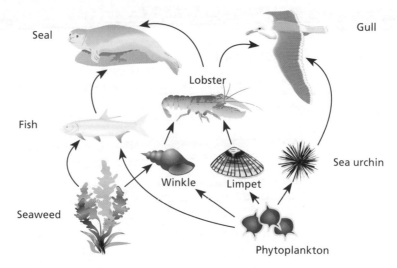

The population of fish in this area of the sea is overfished by people for food.

Suggest, with reasons, **two** effects this could have on other populations of organisms in the food web. **[2 marks]**

1 ....

....

2 ....

....

6 Homeostasis and Response P2 • Grade 4–5

In the 1920s, two scientists called Banting and Best investigated how blood glucose level is controlled.

They removed the pancreas from a dog. The dog could not control the glucose level in its blood.

They then injected an extract from a pancreas into the dog. The dog recovered for a short time.

a) Suggest why the dog recovered, but only for a short time. **[3 marks]**

....

....

....

b) Suggest **one** argument for and **one** argument against this type of experiment. **[2 marks]**

For ....

....

Against ....

....

7 The Rate and Extent of Chemical Change P2 • Grade 4–5 🔺

Magnesium reacts with hydrochloric acid to make hydrogen gas and a soluble salt.

A student wanted to investigate how the concentration of acid affected the rate of reaction.

Suggest **two** methods that could be used to monitor the rate of reaction. **[2 marks]**

1 ....

2 ....

8 Using Resources P2 • Grade 4–5

Jersey is an island in the English Channel.

In 1970, a desalination plant opened to boost the amount of drinking water in times of drought.

Suggest **two** methods Jersey can use to desalinate sea water to provide potable water. **[2 marks]**

1 ....

2 ....

9 Energy P1 • Grade 4–5

A boat has been fitted with a solar panel to supply power for the lights and radio.

a) Suggest why the energy from the solar panel varies from day to day in the
    same week. **[1 mark]**

    ....

b) Suggest why the energy supplied from the solar panel varies at different times
    in the year. **[1 mark]**

    ....

c) Suggest why the electrical system also includes a battery that is charged up
    from the solar panel. **[2 marks]**

    ....

    ....

Total score: .... **/ 24**

Explain

Give reasons for something happening or make the relationships between things clear.

Worked example and more!

TOP TIP
Your answer may involve several sentences and the words 'because' or 'therefore' are often needed.

Example question

1 **Infection and Response P1 • Grade 4–5**

The diagram shows two different types of cell that line the trachea.

Explain how the cells in the diagram protect the lungs from infection by pathogens. **[4 marks]**

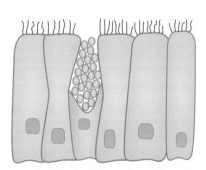

Complete the example

2   Bonding, Structure, and the Properties of Matter ℗ • Grade 4–5

Carbon nanotubes are like a rolled-up sheet of graphene. The figure below shows a carbon nanotube.

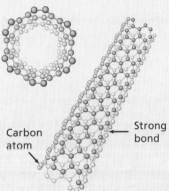

Carbon atom

Strong bond

Explain why carbon nanotubes can conduct electricity.   **[2 marks]**

Carbon nanotubes contain ....

which ....

....

....

3   Electricity ℗ • Grade 4–5 ☺

A student investigated the brightness of lamps in different types of circuit.

The student noticed that when two lamps are connected to a low voltage power supply they are dimmer than if one lamp is connected.

However, the brightness of a single lamp is the same as two lamps connected in a parallel circuit with a low voltage power supply.

Explain these observations.   **[6 marks]**

If lamps are connected in series, the potential difference supplied by the

.... will be divided between the lamps so if there are more

lamps then each of the lamps receives .... and therefore

....

However, if the lamps are connected in parallel, each of the lamps receives

.... This means that if more lamps are

connected then all of them will receive ....

and therefore ....

Exam practice questions

1 Chemical Changes P1 • Grade 1–3

When magnesium is put into a blue Bunsen flame a bright white light is observed. A white powder of magnesium oxide is produced.

Explain why this is an example of an oxidation reaction.

[1 mark]

....

....

2 Energy P1 • Grade 1–3

The photograph shows a lubricant being put onto a bike chain.

Explain why the lubricant is added to the bike chain.

[2 marks]

....

....

....

3 Bioenergetics P1 • Grade 4–5

Rowers need to be very fit.

Rowers have an increased number of mitochondria in their leg muscles and arm muscles.

Runners only have increased numbers of mitochondria in their leg muscles.

Explain this difference.

[3 marks]

....

....

....

....

....

4 Cell Biology ⓟ • Grade 4–5

The picture shows an electron microscope image of *Escherichia coli (E.coli).*

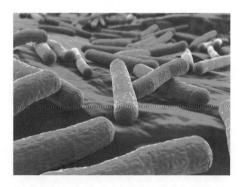

Explain how electron microscopy has increased understanding of sub-cellular structures
in *E.coli*. **[4 marks]**

....

....

....

....

....

5 Organisation ⓟ • Grade 4–5 🔒

A student sets up an experiment about transpiration. They set up four tubes as shown in
the diagram.

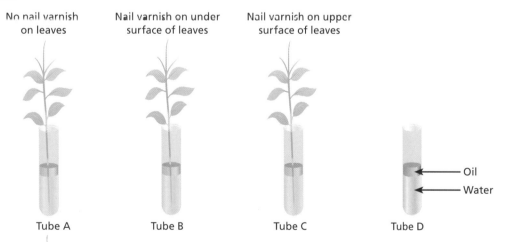

They measure the mass of each tube before and after five days and then calculate the loss in mass.

The table shows the results.

Tube	A	B	C	D
Mass lost in grams	7.0	0.4	6.2	0.0

a) Explain the function of tube **D** in the experiment. **[2 marks]**

....

....

....

b) Explain the difference between the results for tube **B** and tube **C**. **[3 marks]**

....

....

....

....

Homeostasis and Response ⓟ2 • Grade 4–5 🔳

The graph shows information about the number of people needing organ transplants. It also shows the number of dead donors and the number of transplants carried out.

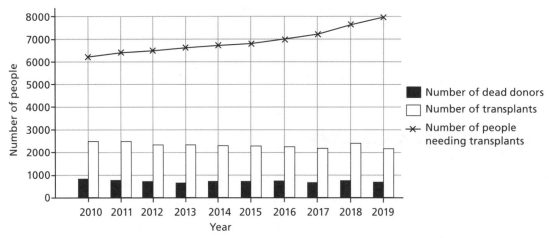

a) More people are being asked to be donors.

Explain why by using the data in the graph. **[2 marks]**

....

....

....

b) There is a difference between the number of dead donors and the number of transplants carried out.

Explain this difference. **[2 marks]**

....

....

7. Atomic Structure and the Periodic Table ⓟ / Bonding, Structure, and the Properties of Matter ⓟ • Grade 4–5

The Periodic Table is a list of all the elements.

Metals are found on the left and towards the bottom of the Periodic Table.

Metals can react with non-metals to make ionic compounds.

a) Explain how metal elements become ions.   [2 marks]

_____

_____

b) Explain how non-metal elements become ions.   [2 marks]

_____

_____

8. Atomic Structure and the Periodic Table ⓟ • Grade 4–5

This question is about groups in the Periodic Table.

a) Explain how the reactivity of Group 1 changes as you go down the group.   [4 marks]

_____

_____

_____

_____

b) Explain how the reactivity of Group 7 changes as you go down the group.   [4 marks]

_____

_____

_____

_____

c) Explain why Group 0 is unreactive.   [1 mark]

_____

_____

9

The Rate and Extent of Chemical Change ⓟ • Grade 4–5

Magnesium metal reacts with hydrochloric acid.

The equation for the reaction is:

magnesium + hydrochloric acid → magnesium chloride + hydrogen

Heating the acid increases the rate of reaction.

Using magnesium powder instead of magnesium ribbon increases the rate of reaction.

a) Explain how increasing the temperature of the acid increases the rate of reaction. **[4 marks]**

b) Explain how using magnesium powder increases the rate of reaction.   **[3 marks]**

10

Forces ⓟ • Grade 4–5

A car is moving at constant speed on a straight, flat road.

Explain why the resultant force = 0.   **[2 marks]**

A student investigated the total resistance in a circuit.

The diagrams show the two circuits that the student used.

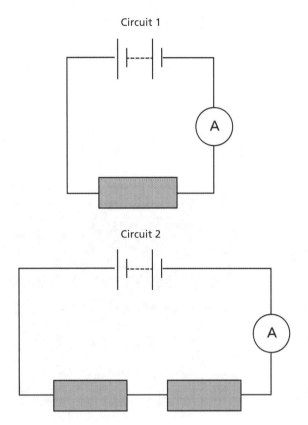

Circuit 1

Circuit 2

Explain the effect of adding resistors in series. **[3 marks]**

....

....

....

....

....

....

Total score: .... **/ 44**

Show

Provide evidence to reach a conclusion. This often involves using mathematics to show that a statement or result is correct.

Worked example and more!

TOP TIP
Make sure you include all the steps leading to the conclusion.

Example question

1 **Electricity P1 • Grade 4–5** 🔢

Show that when a lamp with a resistance of 300 Ω is connected to a power supply with a potential difference of 12 V that the current flowing through the lamp will be 0.04 A.

[3 marks]

Complete the example

2 The Rate and Extent of Chemical Change P2 / Using Resources P2 • Grade 1–3

The Haber process is used to manufacture ammonia.

Ammonia is made from its elements in a reversible reaction.

Show this reversible reaction in a word equation. [2 marks]

_____ + _____ ⇌ _____

3 Infection and Response P1 • Grade 4–5 🖩

Scientists can try to work out how safe drugs are by calculating their therapeutic ratio.

The therapeutic ratio is worked out using this formula:

$$\text{Therapeutic ratio} = \frac{\text{Dangerous dose}}{\text{Smallest dose needed to have an effect}}$$

The table shows data for three drugs, A, B and C.

Drug	Dangerous dose in mg	Smallest dose to have an effect in mg
A	100 000	10 000
B	75	15
C	64	8

The therapeutic ratio can tell a scientist how likely it is for a person to accidentally take a dangerous dose of the drug.

Show that drug A would be the safest drug to use. [2 marks]

The therapeutic ratio for drug A is _____, for drug B it is

_____ and for drug C it is _____.

Therefore, taking drug A would be safest, as it has the _____

_____ ratio so people would be less likely to take a dangerous dose.

Exam practice questions

1 The Rate and Extent of Chemical Change ② • Grade 1–3

Ammonium chloride undergoes thermal decomposition to make ammonia and hydrogen chloride gas.

Show this reversible reaction in a word equation.

[1 mark]

....

2 Chemistry of the Atmosphere ② • Grade 1–3 ▣

The proportions of different gases in the Earth's atmosphere have been the same for about 200 million years.

Approximately, there is 80% nitrogen and the rest is oxygen.

Show that the ratio of nitrogen to oxygen is 4 : 1

[3 marks]

....

....

....

3 Forces ② • Grade 1–3 ▣

Show that a 20 kg mass in the Earth's gravitational field (10 N/kg) has a weight of 200 N.

Use the equation: **weight = mass × gravitational field strength**

[2 marks]

....

....

....

4 Waves ② • Grade 1–3

The diagram shows a wave.

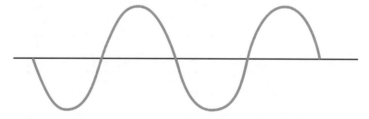

Show the wavelength and amplitude on the diagram.

[2 marks]

5

Ecology ② • Grade 4–5 ▦

The diagram shows the number of units of energy passing through a food chain.

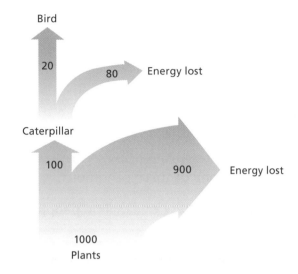

10% of the energy in plants is transferred to the caterpillars.

Show that the transfer of energy from caterpillars to birds is twice as efficient. **[2 marks]**

....

....

....

6

Homeostasis and Response ② • Grade 4–5 ▦

Before In-vitro fertilisation (IVF) fertility treatment, patients have their follicle stimulating hormone (FSH) level measured.

The graph shows information about the FSH levels of patients who then had IVF treatment.

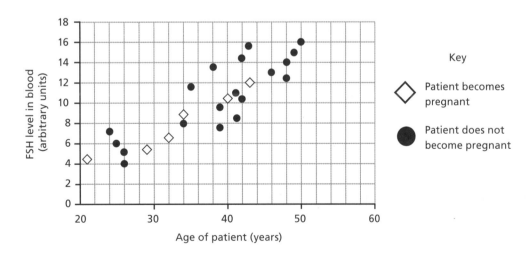

Show that 24% of women who had the IVF treatment became pregnant. **[2 marks]**

....

7 Organisation ⓟ • Grade 4–5 🔢

People were tested for three risk factors for heart disease. They were tested for:

- high blood pressure

- high blood cholesterol

- diabetes.

One million people had at least one of these conditions.

The pie chart shows the results for these one million people.

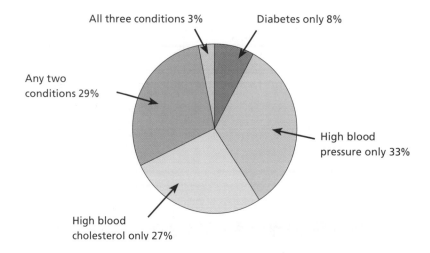

Show that **at least** 360 000 people have high blood pressure. **[2 marks]**

8 Quantitative Chemistry ⓟ • Grade 4–5 🔢 🔒

A student used electrolysis to extract copper metal from copper(II) sulfate solution.
The student calculated that they could obtain a maximum of 63.5 g of copper.
The student collected 15.8 g.

Show that the student collected a 25% yield. **[3 marks]**

9 Quantitative Chemistry P1 / Chemical Changes P1 • Grade 4–5 🖩

Zinc carbonate can undergo thermal decomposition.

The equation for the reaction is:

$ZnCO_3 \rightarrow ZnO + CO_2$

125 g of zinc carbonate was used and the reaction was completed.

Show that 44 g of carbon dioxide was released.

Relative atomic masses (A_r):　　　　C = 12　　　　O = 16　　　　Zn = 65　　　　**[2 marks]**

....

....

10 Bonding, Structure, and the Properties of Matter P1 • Grade 4–5

When a calcium atom bonds with an oxygen atom, two electrons are transferred from the calcium atom to the oxygen atom.

Show the charges on the particles made in this reaction. Tick (✔) the correct box.　　　**[1 mark]**

Ca^{2+} and O^{2+}　　☐

Ca^{2+} and O^{2-}　　☐

Ca^{2-} and O^{2+}　　☐

Ca^{2+} and O^{-}　　☐

11 Bonding, Structure, and the Properties of Matter P1 • Grade 4–5 🖩

The table shows information about three substances, X, Y and Z.

Show the state of each substance at room temperature by filling in the table.　　　**[3 marks]**

Substance	Melting temperature (°C)	Boiling temperature (°C)	State
X	−7	49	
Y	1256	1879	
Z	−180	−160	

12 Forces P2 • Grade 4–5

A 2.5 kg hammer has a weight on the Moon of 4.25 N.

Show that the Moon's gravitational attraction is 1.7 N/kg.   [3 marks]

13 Forces P2 • Grade 4–5

A falling object takes 0.4 seconds to accelerate from rest to a speed of 4 m/s.

Show that the acceleration due to gravity is 10 m/s^2. There are no other forces acting on the object.   [3 marks]

14 Energy P1 • Grade 4–5

A student has two springs, A and B. Spring A has a spring constant of 1000 N/m and spring B has a spring constant of 500 N/m.

Show that using a 2.5 N load causes twice the extension in B than it does in A.   [4 marks]

15 Energy P1 • Grade 4–5

An electric motor is supplied with 500 J of energy as electricity. 125 J is transferred out of the motor as kinetic energy, 325 J as heat and 50 J as sound.

Show that the efficiency of the motor is 25%.   [3 marks]

16 Waves P2 • Grade 4–5 🔲

The note of Middle C has a frequency of 256 Hz. Sound travels at 330 m/s.

Show that the distance between one wave front and the next is 1289 mm to the nearest whole number. **[4 marks]**

....

....

....

....

17 Particle Model of Matter P1 • Grade 4–5 🔲

A rectangular concrete block measures 10 cm × 20 cm × 30 cm and has a mass of 13.5 kg.

Gravitational field strength = 10 N/kg

Show that the density of concrete is 2250 kg/m³. **[4 marks]**

....

....

....

....

Total score: .... **/ 44**

Determine

Use the given data or information to obtain your answer.

Worked example and more!

TOP TIP
The data might be from a graph or table.

Example question

1 Electricity **P1** • Grade 1–3 🖩

Determine the power rating of an electrical heater if the potential difference is 240 V and the current flowing through it is 12 A.

Use the equation:

power = current x potential difference

[3 marks]

Complete the example

In guinea pigs, the allele for black coat, B, is dominant to the allele for brown coat, b.

A brown guinea pig is crossed with a heterozygous black guinea pig.

Determine the expected proportion of brown guinea pigs in the offspring. Use this Punnett square to work out your answer. **[2 marks]**

		Brown parent	
		b	b
Black parent	B	B*b*	
	b		

3 **The Rate and Extent of Chemical Change** ② • Grade 4–5 ▦ 🔒

A student monitored the rate of reaction between hydrochloric acid and magnesium ribbon.

The figure below is a graph of the results.

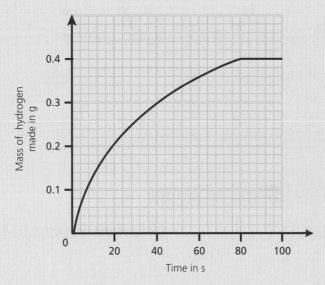

a)   Determine the mean rate of reaction in the first 20 seconds. **[3 marks]**

Mean rate of reaction = change in mass ÷ _____

= _____ ÷ 20   = _____

b)   Determine when the reaction stopped. **[1 mark]**

_____ seconds

Exam practice questions

1 Organic Chemistry P2 • Grade 1–3

Crude oil is a mixture of hydrocarbons.

Crude oil is made mainly of alkanes.

The table shows the names and formulae of the alkanes found in crude oil.

Name	Methane	Ethane	Propane
Formula	CH_4	C_2H_6	C_3H_8

Determine the general formula for alkanes. **[1 mark]**

2 Atomic Structure and the Periodic Table P1 • Grade 1–3

Determine the mass number and the atomic number of the isotope of helium shown below. **[2 marks]**

3 Forces P2 • Grade 1–3 ▦

Determine the weight of a 10 kg block of wood if the gravitational field attraction is 10 N/kg. Use: **weight = mass x gravitational field** **[3 marks]**

4 Homeostasis and Response P2 • Grade 4–5

The table shows some details about problems that can cause infertility in people.

Problem causing infertility	Percentage of infertile couples with this problem
Blocked oviducts	15
Low sperm production	14
No ovulation	7
No sperm made	20
Ovulates irregularly	15
Unknown reason	29

Determine the total percentage of infertile couples where the problem is known to be in the male.

[2 marks]

....%

5 Ecology P2 • Grade 4–5

Sewage can pollute seas and rivers if it is not treated. Scientists think that sewage is leaking into the sea near a beach.

The diagram shows the area next to the sea.

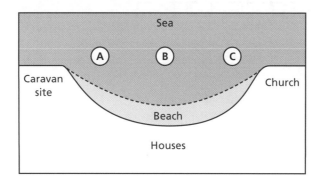

The scientists measure the number of human gut bacteria in the sea at three points, **A**, **B**, and **C**, throughout the summer.

They will have to stop people swimming in the sea if levels of bacteria rise above 1000 in 100 cm³ of sea water anywhere along the beach.

The graph shows their results.

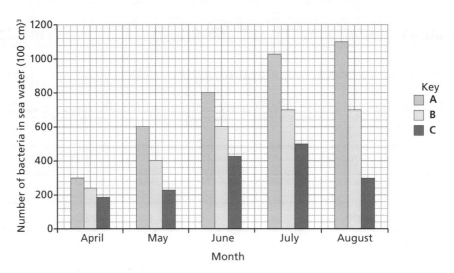

Determine where the sewage is likely to be coming from and when the beach will have to be closed to swimmers. **[2 marks]**

....

....

6 **Bioenergetics P1 • Grade 4–5** 🏠 🔢

The diagram shows an experiment investigating the rate of photosynthesis using pondweed. The graph shows how the rate of photosynthesis changes in response to a change in light intensity.

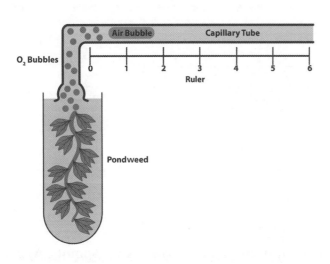

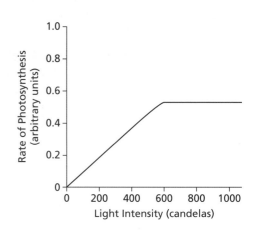

The greater the amount of oxygen produced, the faster the air bubble moves along the capillary tube.

Determine the light intensity needed for maximum rate of photosynthesis.
Use the graph. **[1 mark]**

....

....

7

Ecology ⓟ2 • Grade 4–5 ☺ ▦

Lichens often grow on gravestones. They are very sensitive to acidic gases in the air and cannot survive in polluted air so can be used as an indicator of pollution.

A scientist is investigating lichens growing in three towns, **P, Q** and **R**.
Here are their results.

	Town P	Town Q	Town R
Total number of gravestones looked at	120	100	64
Number of gravestones with lichens	20	20	16

Determine which town is the most polluted. Explain how you worked out your answer.

[3 marks]

....

....

....

....

8

Energy Changes ⓟ1 • Grade 4–5 ☺

A student investigates the reactivity of metals with nitric acid.

This is the method used:

1. Measure 20 cm³ of nitric acid into a polystyrene cup.
2. Measure the temperature of the nitric acid.
3. Add one spatula of metal powder to the nitric acid and stir.
4. Measure the highest temperature the mixture reaches.
5. Calculate the temperature increase for the reaction.
6. Repeat steps 1 to 5 three more times and take an average.
7. Repeat steps 1 to 6 with different metals.

The table shows the results of the experiment.

Metal	Temperature increase in °C				Mean temperature increase in °C
	Trial 1	Trial 2	Trial 3	Trial 4	
Cobalt	6	7	5	9	7
Calcium	54	50	53	55	53
Copper	0	0	0	0	0

a) Determine the independent variable in this experiment. **[1 mark]**

....

b) Determine the unit of the dependent variable in this experiment. [1 mark]

....

c) Determine the order of reactivity for the metals cobalt, calcium and copper. [1 mark]

most reactive ....

....

least reactive ....

9 Chemical Changes P1 • Grade 4–5 📠

Sodium chloride (NaCl) and potassium nitrate (KNO_3) are both salts.

The graph shows the maximum mass of each salt that can dissolve in 100 cm³ of water at different temperatures.

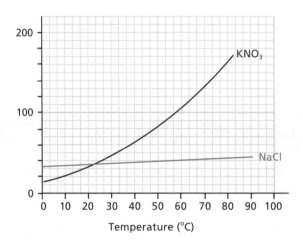

Maximum mass of salt that can dissolve in grams per 100 cm³ of water

a) Determine the temperature when both salts have the same maximum mass dissolved in 100 cm³ of water. [1 mark]

....

b) A student adds potassium nitrate to water at 80°C until no more dissolves.

The student cools 100 cm³ of this solution of potassium nitrate from 80°C to 50°C to produce crystals of potassium nitrate.

Determine the mass of potassium nitrate that crystallises on cooling 100 cm³ of this solution from 80°C to 50°C. [3 marks]

....

....

....

Mass = ... g

10 Electricity ⓟ₁ • Grade 4–5 🖩

Determine the distance travelled by a car which travels at a speed of 40 m/s for one hour.
Give your answer in kilometres (km). **[4 marks]**

....

....

....

.... km

11 Energy ⓟ₁ • Grade 4–5 🖩

Determine the spring constant of a spring which is extended by 10 cm when a mass
of 5 kg is hung from it.

Gravitational field strength = 10 N/kg **[4 marks]**

....

....

....

12 Energy ⓟ₁ • Grade 4–5 🖩

The table contains information about the mass and volume of different objects.

The density of water is 1 g/cm^3.

	Mass (g)	Volume (cm^3)	Will it float? Y/N
Object A	60	40	
Object B	60	80	
Object C	30	80	

Determine whether each object will float or sink in water. Write your answer in the table.

[3 marks]

Total score: .... / 32

Calculate

Use the number values given in the question to work out the answer.

Worked example and more!

TOP TIP
You may need to give your answer in standard form, or to a certain number of decimal places or significant figures.

Example question

1 **Atomic Structure and the Periodic Table P1 • Grade 1–3** ⊞

Sodium is an alkali metal. The figure on the right shows information about one atom of sodium.

Calculate the number of neutrons in one atom of sodium. **[1 mark]**

| 23 |
| Na |
| sodium |
| 11 |

Complete the example

2 Forces P2 • Grade 1-3 ▦

Calculate the average speed of a car that travels a distance of 100 metres in 5 seconds.

Use the equation $s = \frac{d}{t}$ and give your answer in m/s.   **[2 marks]**

$s = d \div t$

$s = 100 \, m \div$

$s =$

3 Cell Biology P1 • Grade 4-5 ▦ 🔒

Some students investigate the effect of the surface area : volume ratio on the rate of diffusion.

They use gelatine cubes stained red with a pH indicator solution.

They put different sized cubes into three different test tubes of hydrochloric acid.

They then time how long it takes for the cubes to completely change colour.

The table shows the results.

Length of each side of cube (mm)	Surface area : volume ratio	Time to completely change colour in seconds	Rate = $\frac{1}{Time}$
2	....	36	....
4	1.5 : 1	60	0.017
6	1 : 1	160	0.0063

a)   Calculate the surface area : volume ratio for the cube with sides 2 mm.   **[3 marks]**

Surface area = 24

Volume = 8

Ratio = ...

b)   Calculate the rate for the cube with sides 2 mm.
Give your answer to 2 significant figures.   **[2 marks]**

1 ÷ 36 =

Rate = ... /second

Exam practice questions

1 Organisation P1 • Grade 1–3 ▦

Blood groups are genetically determined.

There are four main blood groups, O, A, B or AB.

The pie chart shows the percentage of people in the UK with each blood group.

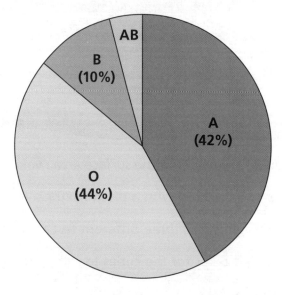

a) Calculate the percentage of people in the UK with blood group AB. **[1 mark]**

b) There are 67 million people in the UK.

   Calculate how many of these people are blood group O. **[2 marks]**

2 Inheritance, Variation and Evolution P2 • Grade 1–3 ▦

A breeding experiment produced 800 pea plants.

Scientists were expecting a ratio of 3 tall plants : 1 dwarf plant.

a) Calculate the percentage of plants that were expected to be tall. **[1 mark]**

Percentage = ...

b) Calculate the number of pea plants that were expected to be dwarf. **[2 marks]**

Number of dwarf plants = ...

3   Electricity ⓟ • Grade 1–3 🖩

Calculate the power rating of a 240 V electric kettle that draws a current of 5 A.

Use the equation:

power = potential difference × current   **[3 marks]**

Give the unit for your answer.

....

....

....

Power rating = ...

4   Cell Biology ⓟ • Grade 4–5 🖩

The table shows the size of different biological structures.

Type of cell	Diameter/length
Cheek cell	70 μm
Red blood cell	7 μm
Salmonella bacterium	1 μm
HIV virus	100 nm

a)   Calculate how many times larger a salmonella bacterium is compared to an HIV virus.

                                                   [2 marks]

....

Answer = ... times

b)   Calculate the number of orders of magnitude between the size of a cheek cell and a red blood cell.   **[1 mark]**

Numbers of magnitude difference = ...

5   Quantitative Chemistry ⓟ • Grade 4–5 🖩

Carbon dioxide, CO_2, is found in small proportions in the air.

Calculate the relative formula mass of carbon dioxide.

Relative atomic masses (A_r):   C = 12   O = 16   **[1 mark]**

....

6 The Rate and Extent of Chemical Change ℗2 • Grade 4–5 🔢 ⏱

A student investigated the rate of reaction between magnesium ribbon and hydrochloric acid.

The figure below shows the equipment used to monitor the reaction.

The starting mass was 404.80 g.

The reaction finished after 90 seconds with the final mass reading 403.65 g.

Calculate the mean rate of reaction.

Give your answer to 3 significant figures. Choose the unit from the box.   **[4 marks]**

g	s/g	g/dm³	mol/dm³	g/s

7 Quantitative Chemistry ℗1 • Grade 4–5 🔢

Calculate the relative formula mass (M_r) of sodium oxide (Na_2O).

Relative atomic masses (A_r): Na = 23, O = 16   **[2 marks]**

8 Forces ℗2 • Grade 4–5 🔢

Calculate the acceleration of a train that speeds up from rest to 50 m/s in 10 seconds.   **[4 marks]**

9   Electricity 🅿1 • Grade 4–5 🔢

Calculate the current flowing through a 100 Ω resistor when a potential difference of 10 V is placed across it.

[4 marks]

....

....

....

....

10   Electricity 🅿1 • Grade 4–5 🔢

Calculate the energy transferred by an 18 W lamp in one hour. Give your answer in kilojoules (kJ).

[3 marks]

....

....

....

Energy transferred = ...

11   Forces 🅿2 • Grade 4–5 🔢

Calculate the kinetic energy of a 15 000 kg bus travelling at 10 m/s.

[4 marks]

....

....

....

Kinetic energy = ...

Total score: .... / 34

Balance

Balance a chemical equation.

Worked example and more!

TOP TIP
Remember there are the same number and type of atoms at the start of the reaction as at the end of the reaction.

Example question

1 Organic Chemistry **P2** • Grade 1–3 🖩

Alkanes can be used as fuels.

Balance the equation for the complete combustion of methane. **[1 mark]**

$$CH_4 + \underline{\quad} O_2 \rightarrow CO_2 + 2H_2O$$

Complete the example

The Haber process is used to manufacture ammonia. Ammonia can be used to make nitrogen-based fertilisers.

Balance the equation for the Haber process. **[1 mark]**

$$N_2 + 3H_2 \rightleftharpoons \underline{\qquad} NH_3$$

Exam practice questions

1 Atomic Structure and the Periodic Table P1 • Grade 1–3 ▦

Group 1 metals react easily with oxygen.

Balance the equation for the oxidation of lithium.

$$\underline{\qquad} Li + O_2 \rightarrow \underline{\qquad} Li_2O$$ **[1 mark]**

2 Organic Chemistry P2 • Grade 4–5 ▦

Ethanol can be used as a fuel.

Balance the symbol equation for the complete combustion of ethanol.

$$C_2H_5OH + \underline{\qquad} O_2 \rightarrow \underline{\qquad} CO_2 + \underline{\qquad} H_2O$$ **[1 mark]**

3 Chemical Changes P1 • Grade 4–5 ▦

Ammonium hydroxide can neutralise sulfuric acid to make a soluble salt.

Balance the equation for this reaction.

$$\underline{\qquad} NH_4OH + \underline{\qquad} H_2SO_4 \rightarrow \underline{\qquad} (NH_4)_2SO_4 + + \underline{\qquad} H_2O$$ **[1 mark]**

4 Atomic Structure and the Periodic Table P1 • Grade 4–5 ▦

Sodium carbonate can react with hydrochloric acid to make a soluble salt, a gas and water.

Balance the equation for this reaction.

$$\underline{\qquad} Na_2CO_3 + \underline{\qquad} HCl \rightarrow \underline{\qquad} NaCl + \underline{\qquad} CO_2 + \underline{\qquad} H_2O$$ **[1 mark]**

Total score: _____ / 4

Measure

Find an item of data from a diagram or photograph. You will probably need to use the measurement to calculate another quantity.

Worked example and more!

TOP TIP
You often have to use your measurement to work out something else, so read the question carefully.

Example question

1 **Electricity** P1 • Grade 1–3 🔒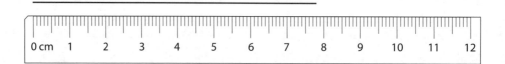

A piece of wire and a scale are shown below.

Measure the length of the wire in cm. **[1 mark]**

0 cm 1 2 3 4 5 6 7 8 9 10 11 12

Complete the example

2 Organisation P1 • Grade 4–5 🔢

The micrograph shows human blood cells.

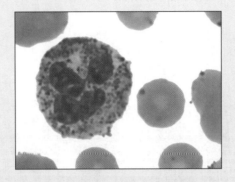

Measure the diameter of the white blood cell and a red blood cell.
Use your measurements to find this ratio:

diameter of a white blood cell : diameter of a red blood cell

Give your answer in the form n : 1.   **[3 marks]**

White blood cell = 26 mm and red blood cell = ...

Ratio = ... : 1

Exam practice questions

1 Organisation P1 • Grade 1–3 🏠

A student wanted to investigate the effect of temperature on enzymes.

The picture shows a thermometer in degrees Celsius.

Measure the temperature on the thermometer.
[1 mark]

.... °C

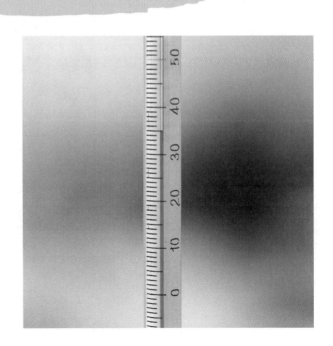

Particle Model of Matter 🅟 • Grade 1–3 😊

A student was measuring the volume of coloured water.

The picture shows the measuring cylinder they used.

Measure the volume of the coloured water.   **[1 mark]**

....cm

Organisation 🅟 • Grade 4–5 🔲

The photograph shows a stomatal pore on the underside of a leaf.

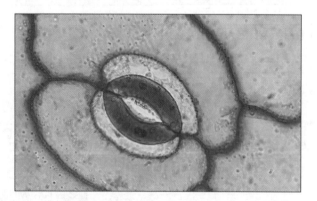

The actual width of the pore is 100 micrometres.

Measure the width of the pore on the image and calculate the magnification of the photograph.

[3 marks]

....

Magnification = × ....

The plant epidermal cell shown below is magnified 250 times.

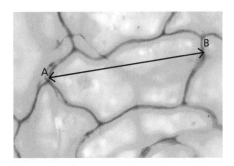

a) Measure the width of the cell using a ruler.   [1 mark]

....

b) Calculate the real width of the cell in mm.

Use the equation:

Real size = $\dfrac{\text{size of image}}{\text{size of real object}}$ [1 mark]

....

c) Calculate the width of the epidermal cell in micrometers (μm).   [1 mark]

....

The diagram shows a palisade cell.

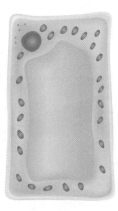

The actual height of the cell is 0.1 mm.

Measure the height of the cell in the diagram and calculate the magnification of the image.   [2 marks]

....

....

6

Cell Biology ⓟ • Grade 4–5 🔢 🏠

A student wants to study cells dividing by mitosis.

They use cells from the tip of a plant root.

They stain the cells with a dye and look at them under a microscope.

The image shows the photograph that the student takes.

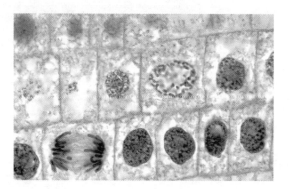

The actual size of each cell is 0.03 mm.

Measure the width of the cell in the photograph and calculate the magnification of the photograph.   **[2 marks]**

....

....

7

Energy ⓟ • Grade 4–5 🔢 🏠

A student wanted to know the specific heat capacity of a metal block.

The picture shows the student measuring the mass of the metal block.

Measure the mass of the metal block in the picture.

Give your answer in kilograms.

Give your answer to 2 significant figures.   **[3 marks]**

....

....

....

....kg

Particle Model of Matter 🅟 • Grade 4–5 🔒

A student was measuring the density of irregular shapes.

They lowered the irregular shapes into a displacement can and collected the water.

The picture shows the measuring cylinder they used to measure the volume of the displaced water.

Measure the volume of the irregular shape.

Give your answer to two significant figures.   **[1 mark]**

....cm

Total score:..................... / 16

Plan

Write a method for carrying out an investigation. This will usually cover one of the required practicals from the specification.

Worked example and more!

TOP TIP
The question may give you hints on what to include in your method or give suggested apparatus.

Example question

1 Organisation **P1** • Grade 4–5 🏠

A person wants to know if sugars or proteins are present in a type of biscuit.

Plan a method that could be used to find out if sugars or proteins are in the biscuits.

[6 marks]

Complete the example

2 Energy P1 • Grade 1–3 😊

Plan how to compare the effectiveness of three different types of insulation material in keeping plastic beakers of hot water hot. You may use a diagram. **[6 marks]**

A diagram showing the equipment and how it will be set up:

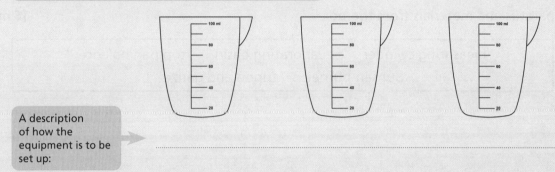

A description of how the equipment is to be set up:

....

....

....

A description of how the equipment will run once it is set up:

....

....

....

A description of what will be done with the data gathered to answer the question:

....

....

....

....

....

3 Chemical Changes P1 • Grade 4–5 😊

A student is given three metals, 1, 2 and 3, to identify. The metals are calcium, zinc and silver.

Plan an investigation to identify the three metals by comparing their reactions with dilute nitric acid. Your plan should give valid results. **[4 marks]**

Add the same mass and .... of metals to the same

.... and concentration of (dilute) nitric acid.

Observe the temperature change or the number of ....

Determine conclusion:

- Silver has no reaction.

- Zinc has some bubbles and .... in temperature.

- Calcium has .... and the ....

  in temperature.

Exam practice questions

46

1 Using Resources P2 • Grade 1–3

Drinking water often contains dissolved salts. The salts can be removed by evaporating the water.

Plan an investigation to measure the mass of the dissolved salts in different samples of drinking water.

Use apparatus and materials from the box.   **[6 marks]**

> measuring cylinder   evaporating basin   top pan balance
> Bunsen burner   tripod and gauze

2 Particle Model of Matter P1 • Grade 1–3

Plan how the volume of an irregular solid could be measured.

You may draw a diagram as part of your answer.   **[4 marks]**

Bioenergetics ⓟ • Grade 4–5 😀

Pondweed is a water plant that can be used to investigate the rate of photosynthesis.

Plan an experiment to investigate how the rate of photosynthesis varies with light intensity. Use this equipment in your investigation.

[6 marks]

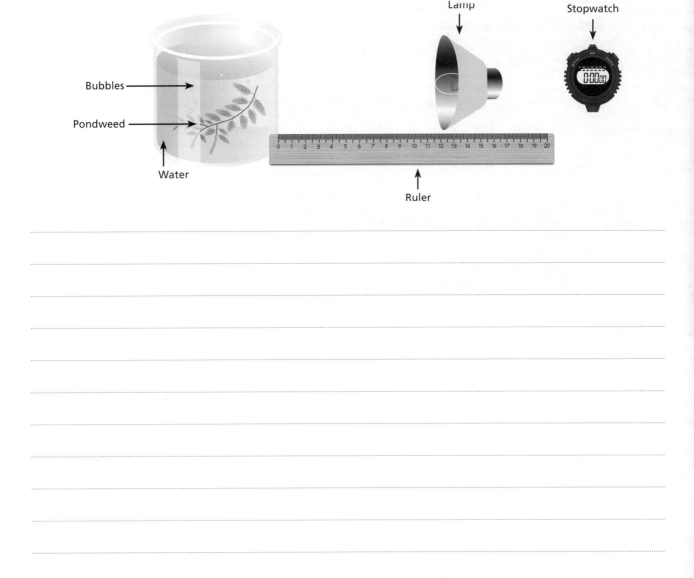

Reaction time in humans is usually between 0.2 s and 0.9 s.

A student wanted to find out whether using the right or left hand of a person would affect their reaction time.

Plan a method for the student's investigation.

Include details of the test you would use for reaction time. **[6 marks]**

....

....

....

....

....

....

....

....

....

....

....

....

....

....

....

Chemical Analysis **P1** • Grade 4–5 📖

Red sweets are made attractive using colourings that contain a dye.

Plan an investigation to determine the R_f value for the red dye in this food colouring.

Your plan should include the use of:
*   a beaker
*   a solvent
*   chromatography paper. **[6 marks]**

6 Chemical Changes ℗ • Grade 4–5 ⌂

Plan a method for making pure dry crystals of copper(II) sulfate crystals from copper(II) oxide and dilute sulfuric acid.

In your method you should name the apparatus you will use.

You do not need to mention safety.   **[6 marks]**

....

....

....

....

....

....

....

....

....

....

7 Particle Model of Matter ℗ • Grade 4–5 ⌂

Plan a valid investigation to determine the density of an irregularly shaped small rock.

In your method you should name the apparatus you will use.

You do not need to mention safety.   **[6 marks]**

....

....

....

....

....

....

....

....

8 Electricity P1 • Grade 4–5

Plan an investigation to determine the relationship between length of wire and resistance.

In your method you should name the apparatus you will use.

You do not need to mention safety. **[6 marks]**

Total score: _____ / 46

Design

Set out how an investigation could be carried out to test a hypothesis. Often this will relate to an experiment or some other type of practical procedure.

Worked example and more!

TOP TIP
Write in a logical sequence and ensure your design would yield useful evidence if it was carried out.

Example question

1 Waves **P2** • Grade 1–3

A student wanted to investigate how the colour of a surface affects the power of the infrared radiation (IR) emitted by the surface.

Design an investigation to compare the amount of infrared radiation emitted by each surface.

Use apparatus and materials from the box.

measuring cylinder   thermometer   kettle   IR detector
conical flask painted black   conical flask painted shiny white

You do not need to include safety information. **[6 marks]**

Complete the example

Two students are on their school football pitch.

One student says that there are more dandelion weeds in the two penalty areas than on the rest of the pitch.

Design an experiment to test this observation. **[6 marks]**

Use a .... to sample the penalty areas.

Place the ....

Count the number of ....

Measure the .... of the penalty areas and calculate the

....

Repeat this process for the ....

.... the numbers from the penalty areas and the rest of the pitch.

Exam practice questions

1 Electricity P1 • Grade 1–3

Design an experiment which explores the relationship between the number of lamps connected in series to a 12 V supply in a circuit and the current flowing in the circuit.   **[6 marks]**

2 Energy P1 • Grade 1–3

Design an experiment to explore the relationship between the gradient of a metre-long ramp and the time taken for a toy car to roll down the ramp starting from rest. The equipment you could use is shown below.   **[4 marks]**

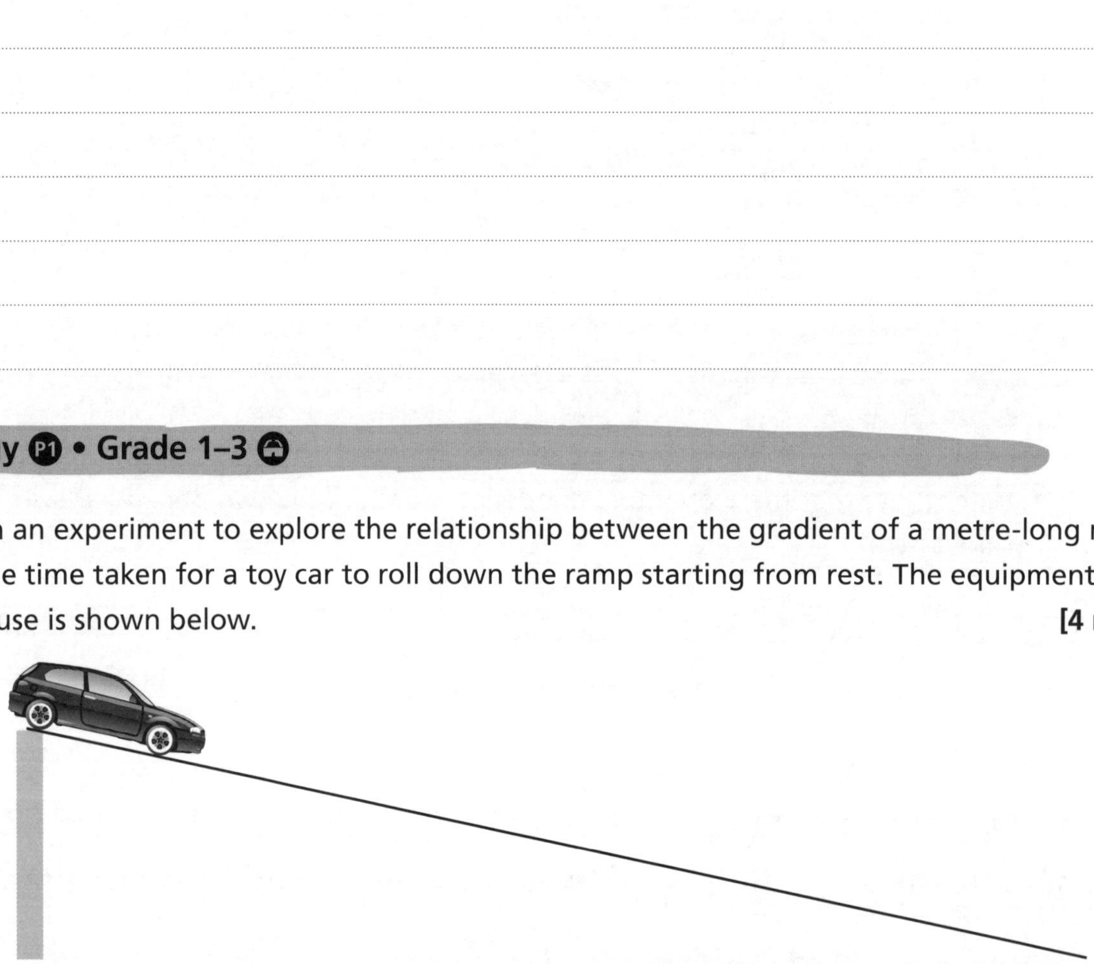

3 Homeostasis and Response P2 • Grade 4–5

Some fizzy cola drinks contain caffeine.

Caffeine is a drug that stimulates the nervous system.

Design an experiment to test the hypothesis that caffeine decreases reaction times.   **[6 marks]**

4 Organisation P1 • Grade 4–5

Cheese is a dairy product high in fat and protein.

A block of cheese contains no starch.

Packaged grated cheese contains starch to prevent the cheese from sticking together in the packet.

Design an experiment to show that a block of cheese doesn't contain starch but grated cheese does.

Give the expected results for this investigation.   **[4 marks]**

5 | Organisation ℗ • Grade 4–5 🏠

Amylase is an enzyme found in the mouth.

Amylase breaks down starch into simple sugars.

Design an experiment to show the effect of pH on the rate of enzyme action of amylase.

You do not need to include safety information. **[4 marks]**

6 | Particle Model of Matter ℗ • Grade 4–5 🏠

This bolt is around 5 cm long and is made from metal.

Design a procedure to find the density of the bolt.

Include the equipment that you would use.

Describe the measurements that you would take and the calculations you would do.

You do not need to include safety information. **[6 marks]**

7   Forces P2 • Grade 4–5

Some students have been measuring reaction times using a 30 cm ruler. The ruler is held vertically and released by one person, whilst another person grips it as soon as they see it fall.

Design an experiment to find out the effect of drinking an energy drink on reaction times.   **[6 marks]**

Total score: _____ **/ 36**

Plot

Construct a graph on a printed grid using data given in the question.

TOP TIP
If you are asked to draw a line of best fit, this could be a smooth curve or one straight line.

Example question

1 **Homeostasis and Response P2 • Grade 1–3** 🖩 ⏱

The table shows the results of an experiment to measure the effect on reaction time of having different numbers of alcoholic drinks.

Number of drinks	0	1	2	3	4	5	6
Reaction time in seconds	0.2	0.3	0.5	0.8	1.4	1.9	2.6

Plot the data on the grid. Include a line of best fit. **[3 marks]**

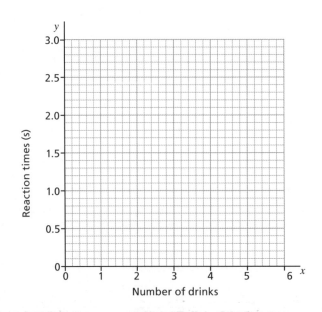

Complete the example

2 The Rate and Extent of Chemical Change ⓟ • Grade 4–5 🔳 🔒

Sodium thiosulfate solution reacts with dilute hydrochloric acid to form a cloudy solution.

A student is investigating how the concentration of sodium thiosulfate affects the rate of reaction.

The student uses the equipment shown.

The table shows the results.

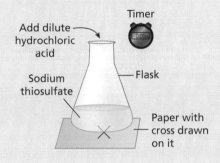

Concentration (arbitrary units)	Time (s)
10	180
20	100
30	70
40	50
50	45
60	40
70	35

Plot the data from the table on the graph below.   **[2 marks]**

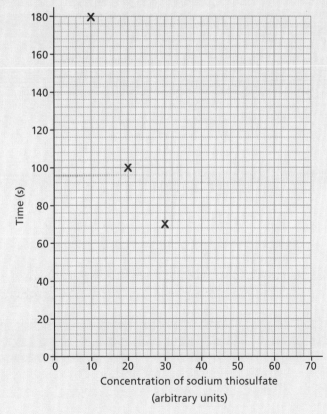

A student measured their journey to school.

The table records the time and distance the student travelled.

Time (minutes)	0	1	2	3	4	5	6	7	8
Distance (km)	0	0.1	0.2	0.3	0.3	0.3	0.4	0.5	0.6

Plot a distance–time graph of the student's journey. **[2 marks]**

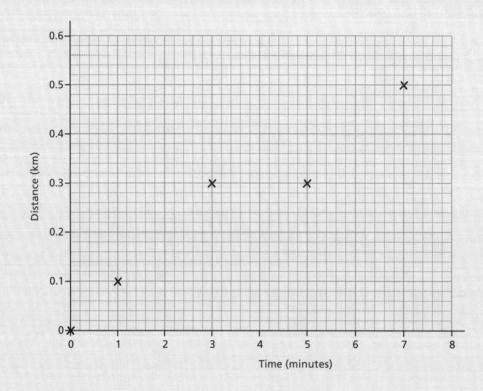

Exam practice questions

1 **Bioenergetics P1 • Grade 1–3** 🔢 ⬆

In a photosynthesis experiment, a student put a lamp at different distances from some pondweed.

They then measured the number of bubbles given off by the pondweed in one minute at each distance.

The table shows their results.

Distance of lamp from pondweed in cm	Number of bubbles per minute
10	40
20	30
40	16
50	12
70	10

Plot these results on the grid. Include a line of best fit. **[3 marks]**

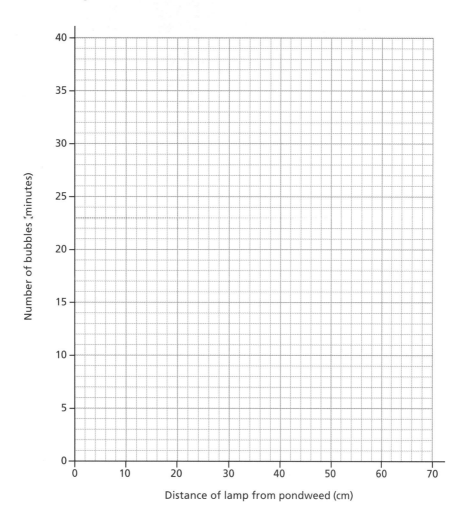

Building materials have different densities.

The table below shows the densities of some common building materials.

Material	Density (g/cm³)
Concrete	2.0
Steel	8.0
Brick	2.5

Plot the density of brick on the graph. **[1 mark]**

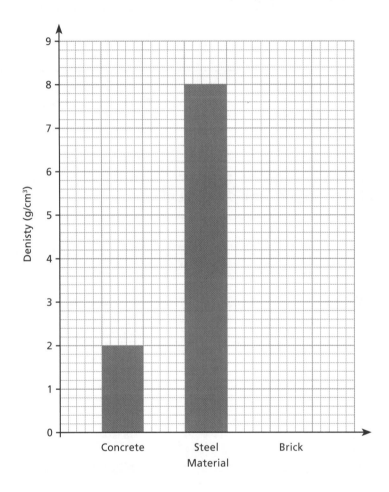

Some students investigate plants growing near a tree.

They use a quadrat to measure the percentage of ground covered by plants at different distances from the tree.

The table shows their results.

Distance from the tree in metres	Percentage of ground covered by plants
1	10
2	14
3	18
4	26
5	52
6	60
7	62

Plot these results on the grid.

Include a line of best fit. **[5 marks]**

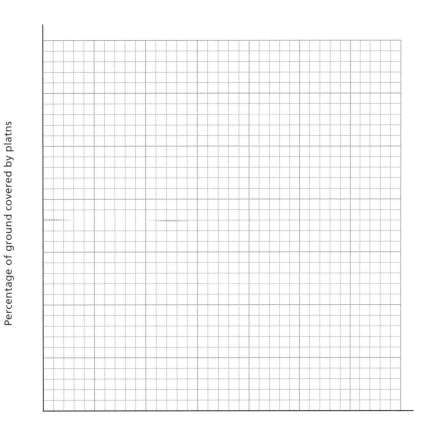

Distance from the trees in metres

Magnesium reacts with dilute hydrochloric acid to form hydrogen gas.

A student is investigating how the mass changes during the reaction. The student uses the equipment shown in the figure. The table shows the student's results.

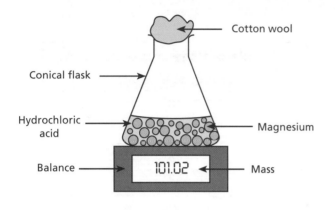

Time (s)	Mass (g)
0	200
20	188
40	176
60	168
80	161
100	155
120	151

Plot the data from the table on the graph below.   **[2 marks]**

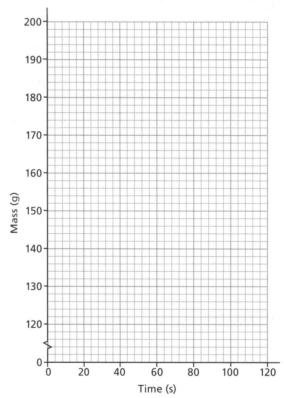

Energy ⓟ • **Grade 4–5** 🔲 🏠

This data shows the load on a spring and the extension caused.

Plot a graph showing the relationship between these variables.

[4 marks]

Load/N	0	1	2	3	4	5	6	7
Extension/mm	0	3	6	10	13	17	20	24

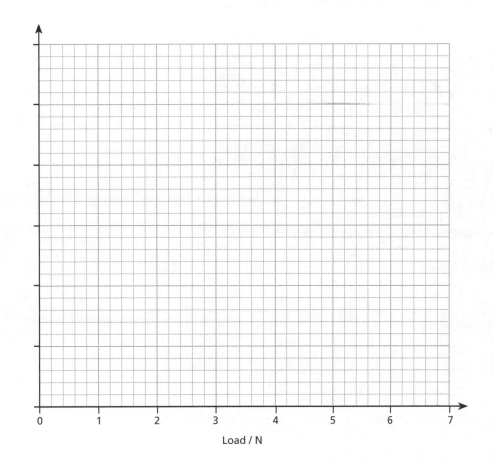

Load / N

Total score: .... **/ 15**

Compare

Describe the similarities and/or differences between two things, rather than writing about one.

Worked example and more!

TOP TIP
Make sure your answers actually compare the features and do not just write about each one separately.

Example question

1 Magnetism and Electromagnetism P2 • Grade 4–5

A student has two rectangular pieces of metal, with similar dimensions. One is a permanent magnet and the other is a piece of magnetic metal.

Compare the two objects in terms of what will happen when another permanent magnet is brought near to first one wond then the other. **[4 marks]**

Complete the example

2 Bonding, Structure, and the Properties of Matter ⓟ • Grade 1–3

Covalent bonds hold the atoms together in a water molecule.

There are intermolecular forces of attraction between different water molecules.

The figure shows a diagram of water molecules interacting.

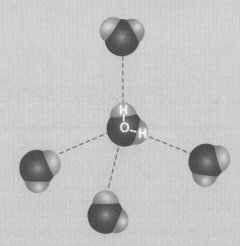

Compare the strength of covalent bonds to intermolecular forces.

Tick (✓) **one** box.   **[1 mark]**

> Think about how much energy would be needed to separate the oxygen and hydrogen atoms in a molecule of water. Compare this to how much energy would be needed to overcome the intermolecular forces when melting ice (solid water) into liquid water.

Covalent bonds are weaker than intermolecular forces.   ☐

Covalent bonds are the same strength as intermolecular forces. ☐

Covalent bonds are stronger than intermolecular forces.   ☐

3 Bioenergetics ⓟ • Grade 4–5

Compare the processes of aerobic respiration and anaerobic respiration in muscle cells.   **[5 marks]**

Both of these reactions supply energy for _____ .

They are both _____ reactions and use _____ .

Aerobic respiration needs _____ , but anaerobic respiration does not.

Anaerobic respiration produces _____ , but aerobic

respiration produces _____ .

_____ is released by anaerobic respiration.

Exam practice questions

1 The Rate and Extent of Chemical Change **P2** • Grade 1–3

A student investigated the rate of reaction between magnesium metal and hydrochloric acid.

The student completed the experiment with magnesium ribbon.

The sketch graph shows the results.

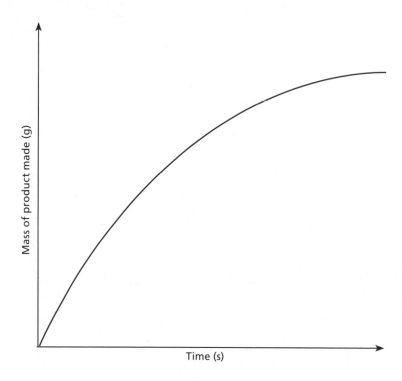

Compare the line of best fit for magnesium ribbon with magnesium powder.

Tick (✔) **one** box.

The line of best fit for a higher surface area would have a less steep slope. ☐

The line of best fit for a higher surface area would have slopes with the same steepness. ☐

The line of best fit for a higher surface area would have a steeper slope. ☐

[1 mark]

2 Energy P1 • Grade 1–3

A student is choosing a pocket calculator to buy. One of these is battery powered and the other uses photovoltaic cells to capture energy from light to power it.

Compare these two devices. **[4 marks]**

....

....

....

....

....

....

3 Electricity P1 • Grade 1–3

This question is about electrical current.

Compare alternating and direct flows of current in a circuit. **[2 marks]**

....

....

....

....

....

4 Electricity P1 / Magnetism and Electromagnetism P2 • Grade 1–3

The National Grid transfers electrical power from power stations to consumers.

Step-up and step-down transformers are part of the National Grid.

Compare the two types of transformer. **[2 marks]**

....

....

....

....

....

5 Organisation P1 • Grade 4–5

Compare the diseases AIDS and gonorrhoea.

In your answer include:
- the type of pathogen involved
- how the disease is spread and how this can be prevented
- how the disease is treated.

[5 marks]

....

....

....

....

....

....

....

....

....

....

....

6 Cell Biology P1 • Grade 4–5

In a living organism, cells must grow and divide to make new cells.

Mitosis and meiosis are the two different processes by which cells can divide and make new cells.

Compare the processes of mitosis and meiosis.

[5 marks]

....

....

....

....

....

....

....

....

....

....

....

7 Cell Biology P1 • Grade 4–5

Plant roots absorb mineral ions and water.

Water is absorbed by osmosis and mineral ions are absorbed by active transport.

Compare the two processes to absorb substances into the roots of plants. **[4 marks]**

....

....

....

....

....

....

8 Bioenergetics P1 • Grade 4–5

Compare the processes of aerobic respiration and anaerobic respiration
in muscle cells. **[5 marks]**

....

....

....

....

....

....

9 Bonding, Structure, and the Properties of Matter P1 • Grade 4–5

The table shows the structure of three different forms of carbon.

Substance	Graphite	Diamond	Buckminsterfullerene
Structure			

Compare the structure and bonding of the different forms of carbon. **[4 marks]**

The diagrams show the structures of two alkane molecules.

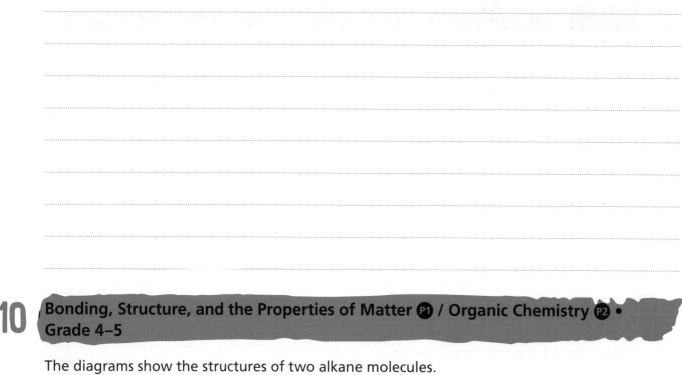

Ethane   Pentane

The table shows the melting and boiling point values for these two alkanes.

Alkane	Melting point (°C)	Boiling point (°C)
Ethane	−183	−89
Pentane	−130	36

Compare the structure and properties of ethane and pentane. **[6 marks]**

Potable water is water which is safe to drink.

The first stage of making potable water is to select a suitable source.

The second stage is to treat it to ensure it has sufficiently low levels of dissolved salts and microbes.

Compare how easily potable water can be obtained from:

- fresh water (ground water, lake water and river water)

- waste water (sewage). **[6 marks]**

Total score: .... / 44

Estimate

Find an approximate value.

Worked example and more!

TOP TIP
It may be a calculation where the result is not exact but based on sampling, or it could involve a graph where you need to find an approximate value.

Example question

1 **Atomic Structure and the Periodic Table P1 • Grade 1–3 🖩**

Group 1 metals are all solids at room temperature.

The table shows the melting point of the Group 1 metals.

Element	Lithium	Sodium	Potassium	Rubidium
Melting point (°C)	180	98	63	39

Estimate the melting point of francium. **[1 mark]**

Complete the example

2 Bioenergetics P1 • Grade 4–5

The photo shows a racehorse. When a racehorse runs, its heart rate increases.

The graph shows data about the heart rate of a horse when it is running at different speeds.

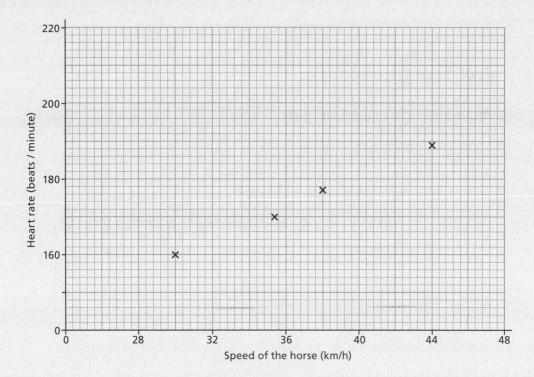

When the heart rate of a horse is above 200 beats per minute, the horse starts to rely on anaerobic respiration.

Estimate the maximum speed the horse can run without relying on anaerobic respiration. Show on the graph how you worked out your answer. **[3 marks]**

In this question, you first need to draw a line of best fit on the graph using the four points. It should be a straight line in this case. Make sure you extend the line so you can read off the speed at 200 beats per minute.

Speed = ... km per hour

3 Energy P1 • Grade 4–5

This diagram shows a block of wood floating in water.

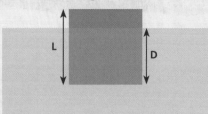

Estimate the percentage of the wood that is submerged. **[4 marks]**

> Imagine the height of the block to have a value of 100, then consider what the height under water would be. If the whole block is 100, the submerged part looks to be about 80, so 80% is a reasonable answer.

The percentage submerged is the amount of the whole

that is under the surface of the _____ . By comparing this

with the _____ , this will be around _____ %.

Exam practice questions

⏱ 18

1 Organic Chemistry P2 • Grade 1–3 ▣

Alkanes are hydrocarbons found in crude oil.

The table shows some information about alkanes.

Alkane	Molecular formula	Boiling point (°C)
Methane	CH_4	−162
Ethane	C_2H_6	−89
Propane	C_3H_8	−42

Butane is the next alkane in the series. Butane is a gas at room temperature.

Estimate the boiling point of butane. **[1 mark]**

2 Forces P2 • Grade 1–3 ▣

A ramp has been set up to enable the motion of a trolley to be investigated.

Look at the ramp and also the image of the protractor.

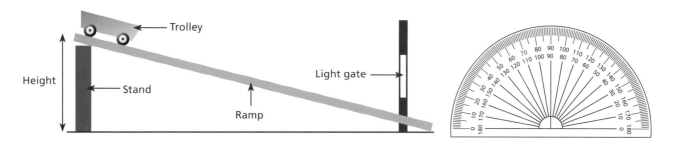

Estimate the angle between the surface of the ramp and the horizontal. **[1 mark]**

---

3 Ecology ⓟ2 • Grade 4–5 🔢 ⌂

Some students investigate beetles living in an area of the school grounds.

They use a method called capture-recapture to estimate the population size of the beetles. They catch beetles from the area, count them, mark them, and then let them go. This is the first sample.

The next day they catch beetles from the area again. This is the second sample.

The table shows their results.

Number of beetles caught in the first sample	18
Number of beetles caught in the second sample	10
Number of beetles caught in the second sample that were previously marked	4

Estimate the population of beetles in the area.

Use this formula to work out your answer. **[2 marks]**

$$\text{Population size} = \frac{\text{number in 1st sample} \times \text{number in 2nd sample}}{\text{number in 2nd sample previously marked}}$$

Population size = ...

4 Ecology ⓟ2 • Grade 4–5 🔢 ⌂

Some students are investigating how many mosquito larvae live in their school pond.

They put a quadrat on the surface of the pond and count the number of mosquito larvae inside the quadrat.

They do this four times in different places on the pond's surface.

The table shows the results.

	Quadrat 1	Quadrat 2	Quadrat 3	Quadrat 4
Number of larvae	12	10	7	11

The area of each quadrat is 0.25 m² and the area of the pond is 12 m².

Estimate the total number of mosquito larvae in the pond. **[3 marks]**

5 **Ecology ② • Grade 4–5 🔒 🧮**

A student wanted to estimate the population of buttercup plants in a field.

This is the method used:

1. Randomly place a 1 m² quadrat on the field.

2. Count and record the number of whole buttercup plants in the quadrat.

3. Repeat steps 1 and 2 until ten sets of data have been collected.

The mean number of buttercups in each quadrat was 6.2.

The area of the field was 50 m by 100 m.

Estimate the population of the buttercups in the field. **[2 marks]**

Estimated population of buttercups in the field = ...

6 **Atomic Structure and the Periodic Table ① • Grade 4–5 🧮**

The bar chart shows the densities of some alkali metals.

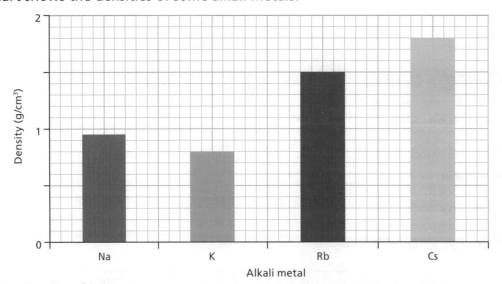

Estimate the density of lithium. **[1 mark]**

7 Atomic Structure and the Periodic Table ⓟ • Grade 4–5 🔢

Halogens are non-metal elements.

The table shows the boiling point of the Group 7 halogens.

Element	Boiling point (°C)
Fluorine	−188
Bromine	60
Iodine	184
Astatine	337

Estimate the boiling point of chlorine. [1 mark]

....

8 Using Resources ⓟ • Grade 4–5 🔢

Alloys are chemical formulations which are often more useful than a pure metal.

Steel is an alloy mainly made of iron with other elements added.

The pie chart shows the composition of stainless steel.

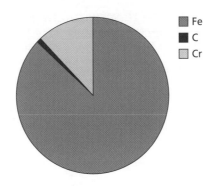

■ Fe
■ C
■ Cr

a) Estimate the percentage of iron in stainless steel. [1 mark]

....

b) Estimate the fraction of chromium in stainless steel. [1 mark]

....

9 Waves ⓟ2 • Grade 4–5 🏠

A student is studying waves and needs to know their wavelength. Look at the image of the waves and a ruler.

Estimate the wavelength of the waves. **[1 mark]**

10 Energy ⓟ1 • Grade 4–5 🏠

Estimate the temperature shown on this thermometer. **[1 mark]**

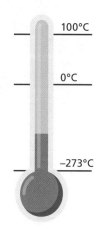

11 Electricity ⓟ • Grade 4–5

A diode will allow current to flow in one direction but not in the other direction.

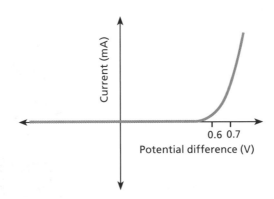

Estimate the voltage at which current starts to flow through the diode when the potential difference is applied in the correct direction to the diode. **[1 mark]**

12 Forces ⓟ₂ • Grade 4–5 ▦

A group of students are exploring how an elastic band stretches when it is loaded.

They suspend the elastic band from a clamp stand, hang a carrier from the elastic band and add masses to the carrier.

They measure from the top of the elastic band to the bottom of the carrier each time they add another weight.

The results are shown in the table.

Force applied by adding masses (N)	0	0.2	0.4	0.6	0.8
Length of elastic band and carrier (cm)	10	10.8	11.6	12.0	13.2
Extension cased by adding masses (cm)	0	0.8	1.6	2.4	3.2

Estimate the extension that would have been caused by a force of 0.7 N. **[1 mark]**

Total score: _____ / 18

Predict

Give a plausible outcome or result.

Worked example and more!

TOP TIP
A prediction doesn't have to be what will actually happen but it should show your scientific knowledge and understanding.

Example question

1 **Forces P2 • Grade 1–3**

A toy car is rolled down a 1 m ramp.

a) Predict the speed of the vehicle as it rolls down the ramp.
Use ideas about forces in your answer. **[2 marks]**

b) Predict the speed of the vehicle as it rolls across the floor.
Use ideas about forces in your answer. **[2 marks]**

Complete the example

2 Atomic Structure and the Periodic Table P1 • Grade 4–5

Halogens are Group 7 elements. The table gives information about the physical appearance of the halogens at room temperature.

Halogen	Physical appearance at room temperature
Fluorine	Pale yellow gas
Chlorine	Pale green gas
Bromine	Brown liquid
Iodine	Grey solid
Astatine	

Predict the physical appearance of astatine.   **[2 marks]**

> There is 1 mark for the colour and 1 mark for the correct state at room temperature.

Exam practice questions

1 Chemical Changes P1 • Grade 1–3 🏠

A student investigated the electrolysis of copper(II) sulfate solution. The figure shows a diagram of the equipment used.

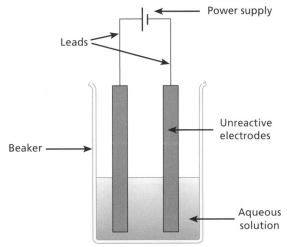

Bubbles of gas were collected at the positive electrode.

a) Predict the observation at the negative electrode.   **[1 mark]**

b) Predict how the colour of the solution would change during electrolysis.   **[2 marks]**

2 Atomic Structure and the Periodic Table Ⓟ❶ • Grade 1–3

Iron can react with halogens to make iron(III) halides.

The table shows the results of these reactions.

Halogen	Observation
Fluorine	Violent reaction with bright flame
Chlorine	A fast reaction with an orange flame
Bromine	A quick reaction with an orange glow

a) Predict what you would observe when iodine reacts with iron. **[1 mark]**

b) Predict the product of the reaction between chlorine and iron. **[1 mark]**

3 The Rate and Extent of Chemical Change Ⓟ❷ • Grade 4–5 ⬆ ▦

A student investigated the rate of reaction between hydrochloric acid and magnesium ribbon.

The graph shows their results.

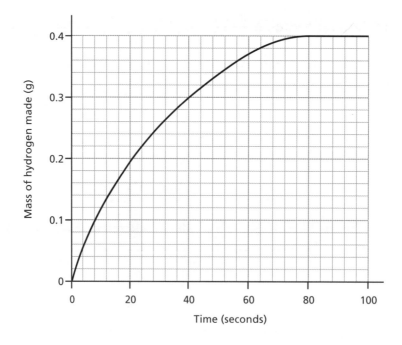

Predict the time taken for the reaction to be complete.

Give your answer in minutes.

Give your answer to three significant figures.   **[3 marks]**

....

....

....

4 The Rate and Extent of Chemical Change P2 • Grade 4–5 😊

A student investigated the rate of reaction between magnesium ribbon and hydrochloric acid.

The equipment used and a graph of the results are shown below.

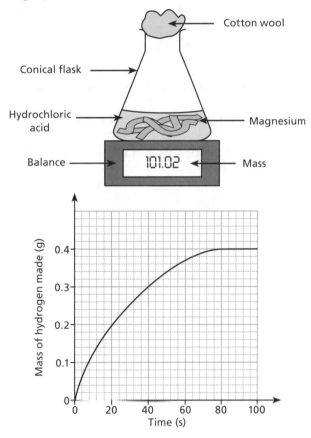

The reaction was monitored for 100 seconds and there was magnesium left behind.

a) Predict the effect on the rate of reaction if a higher concentration of
    hydrochloric acid was used.   **[1 mark]**

....

b) Predict the effect on the maximum mass of hydrogen produced if magnesium
    powder was used instead of magnesium ribbon.   **[1 mark]**

....

....

c) Predict the effect of increasing the temperature.   **[1 mark]**

....

5 The Rate and Extent of Chemical Change ② • Grade 4–5 ☺

In the 'disappearing cross' experiment, hydrochloric acid reacts with sodium thiosulfate.

One of the products of the reaction is sulfur, which is insoluble.

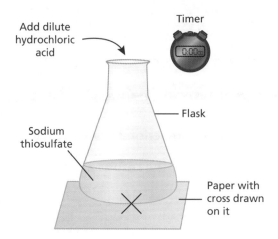

A student carries out the experiment using 36.5 g//dm³ of acid.

They add the acid to the sodium thiosulfate and time how long it takes for the cross to disappear.

They then repeat the experiment with the acid at half and quarter concentration.

Temperature could affect the rate of reaction, so the same temperature must be used for each part of the investigation.

Predict and explain how increasing the temperature would affect the time taken for the cross to disappear.   **[2 marks]**

....

....

....

6 Energy ① • Grade 4–5

Two cups of coffee are poured at the same time into identical cardboard cups and one of them has a plastic lid placed on top.

The volumes and temperature of coffee are the same.

Predict which cup of coffee will cool down quicker and suggest why.   **[2 marks]**

....

....

....

....

7 **Particle Model of Matter** ⓟ① • **Grade 4–5**

A beaker has equal volumes of water and oil placed in it.

The water has a density of 1 g/cm³ and the oil has a density of 0.85 g/cm³.

The liquids don't mix but settle out as separate layers.

Predict which layer will be on top and suggest why. **[2 marks]**

....

....

8 **Forces** ⓟ② • **Grade 4–5** 🔄

Some students are exploring how gravity affects motion.

The velocity–time graph shows the motion of a stone dropped from a height and falling towards the ground.

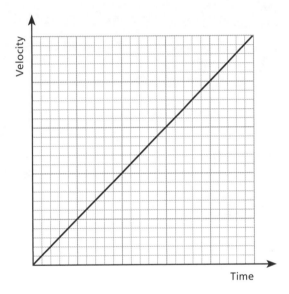

The students now attach a small parachute made of polythene sheet and pieces of cotton to the stone and release it from the same height above the ground.

Predict the motion of the stone by drawing another line on the graph showing what its descent will now be. Explain your answer. **[2 marks]**

....

....

Total score: .... **/ 19**

Evaluate

Use the information supplied, as well as your knowledge and understanding, to consider evidence for and against when making a judgement / claim.

Worked example and more!

TOP TIP
Consider questions such as:
• What is the judgement?
• How is it supported and opposed by evidence?
• How well is the evidence connected to the judgement?

Example question

1 **Organisation P1 • Grade 4–5**

A student designed an investigation to find the optimum temperature for amylase to work.

This is their method:

• Add 1 cm³ of amylase to 5 cm³ starch solution in a test tube.
• Place this tube in a water bath at 20°C and start timing.
• Every 30 seconds take a sample and test for starch.
• Note the time that the starch test gives a negative result.
• Repeat with the water bath at 30, 40, 50 and 60°C.

The table shows the student's results.

Temperature of the water bath in °C	20	30	40	50	60
Time taken for a negative starch test in seconds	210	120	90	150	300

The student concluded that the optimum temperature for amylase is 40°C.

Evaluate the student's conclusion. Refer to the method in your answer. **[4 marks]**

Complete the example

2 Chemical Changes P1 • Grade 4–5

The picture shows zinc (Zn).
Zinc is a metal.

It is extracted from zinc oxide (ZnO).

All other solid products from the extraction method must be separated from the zinc.

The table shows information about three possible methods to extract zinc from zinc oxide.

Method	Reactant	Relative cost	Products
1	Hydrogen gas	High	Zinc solid Water gas
2	Coke	Low	Zinc solid Carbon dioxide gas
3	Aluminium	Low	Zinc solid Aluminium oxide solid

Evaluate the three possible methods for extracting zinc from zinc oxide. **[4 marks]**

Carbon and _____ are cheaper reactants than hydrogen, which

_____ .

However, there is a financial and time cost for removing a solid product

such as _____

from the zinc, which is not needed when _____

or _____ are used. So,

_____ would be the best method.

A teacher presents a class of students with a model showing what happens when current flows around a circuit.

The teacher uses a continuous loop of cord and has a group of students holding the cord loosely so it can pass through their hands. The teacher is gripping the cord and makes it move around through the students' hands.

The teacher suggests that it is rather like when a power supply makes a current flow.

Evaluate the strengths and weaknesses of this model. **[6 marks]**

The model is an effective one because it shows that charged particles

originate in the circuit and don't all start from   .

It also shows that these particles all set off in motion

                                                            .

The model shows that the current flow is the same

                                        . If one of the pupils starts to grip

the cord harder, their hand will get warmer due to friction and this shows

how   . However,

the model only works for a series

and it is also inaccurate because

                                        . Overall, the value of the model

is   .

Exam practice questions

1 | **Electricity P1 • Grade 1–3**

The picture shows information about three types of lamps. These include LED (light emitting diode), CFL (compact fluorescent lamps) and incandescent (or filament) lamps.

Incandescent	**CFL**	**LED**
Average life span: 1,200 hrs	Average life span: 8,000 hrs	Average life span: 25,000 hrs
60 Watts	Mercury	No Mercury
	13–15 Watts (60 W equivalent)	6–8 Watts (60 W equivalent)
	Uses 75% less energy	Uses 84% less energy

Evaluate the information provided and suggest which type you would use in your home and why.

[4 marks]

....

....

....

....

....

....

....

....

The coronary artery supplies the heart muscle with blood.

A new technique has been developed to measure the internal diameter of the coronary artery.

Twelve men had their coronary arteries measured. Six of the men were healthy and the other six had heart disease.

The results are shown in the graph.

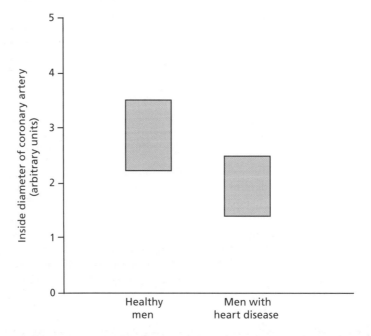

A newspaper claims that this technique can be used to predict heart disease in all patients.

Evaluate this claim using the information in the method, the graph and your own knowledge. **[5 marks]**

....

....

....

....

....

....

....

....

....

....

Graph A gives information about the mass of butter and margarine eaten in the USA between 1910 and 2010.

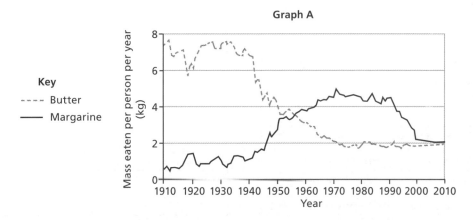

Graph B gives information about the number of people in the USA who died from heart disease between 1910 and 2010.

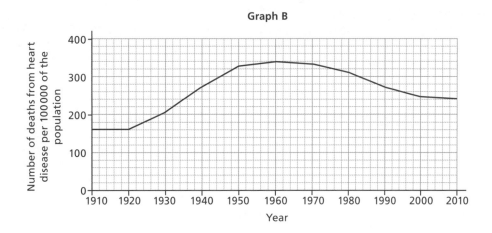

A student says that the graphs show that butter is a healthier food than margarine.

Evaluate this statement using information from **Graph A** and **Graph B**.   **[6 marks]**

....

....

....

....

....

....

....

....

....

....

4   Using Resources P2 • Grade 4–5

The table shows information about two different materials used to make drinks bottles.

	Glass	Plastic
Raw material	Sand, limestone, salt	Crude oil
Bottle material	Soda-lime glass	Polypropene
Maximum temperature used in production	1600°C	850°C
Number of times reused	25	0
Percentage of recycled material used in new bottles	50	10
Fossil fuel use to produce and transport (arbitrary units)	4320	2639

Evaluate the sustainability of the production of drinks bottles made from soda-lime glass and polypropene.

Use the table and your own knowledge. **[6 marks]**

....

....

....

....

....

....

....

....

....

....

5   Using Resources P2 • Grade 4–5

The carbon footprint is the total amount of carbon dioxide and other greenhouse gases emitted over the full life cycle of a product, service or event.

The table shows the carbon footprint for the manufacturing of three bicycles.

Two of the bicycles are e-bikes and one is a push bike.

Bicycle	Mass of CO_2 produced during manufacture in kg	Mass of CO_2 produced when driving in kg per km	Total mass of CO_2 produced from manufacture and 1000 km use in kg	Total mass of CO_2 produced from manufacture and average lifetime use in kg
Bicycle A	116	0	116	116
Bicycle B	134	0.025	159	614
Bicycle C	165	0.02	365	549

Evaluate the carbon footprint of the bicycles.

Use information from the table. **[6 marks]**

....

....

....

....

....

....

....

....

....

....

6 **Forces P2 • Grade 4–5 ⊕**

Some students are exploring the motion of a trolley on a ramp. The ramp is at a gradient and when the students release the trolley at the top they can see it accelerates. There are lines across the ramp at 10 cm intervals.

The ramp is 1 m long and they want to see how long it takes to travel each 10 cm section. One student suggests that a good way of doing this would be to use their phone to video record the motion of the trolley as it goes down.

Evaluate this as a way of gathering evidence about the motion of the trolley. **[6 marks]**

....

....

....

....

....

....

....

....

....

Total score: .... **/ 33**

Justify

Support a case or argument with evidence. This evidence is usually from data provided in the question.

Worked example and more!

TOP TIP
Unlike 'Evaluate' questions, you do not need to give arguments for and against.

Example question

1 **Organisation P1 • Grade 1–3** 🔢

Scientists investigate the effect of pH on the rate of reaction of enzyme **A** and enzyme **B**.

The graph shows their results.

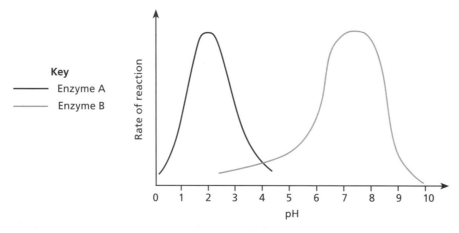

The scientists claim that enzyme **A** is found in the stomach and enzyme **B** is found in the small intestine.

Justify the scientists' claim. **[4 marks]**

Complete the example

The model of the structure of the atom has changed over time.

In one experiment, positively charged alpha radiation was fired at a sheet of very thin gold foil. The diagram shows the experiment.

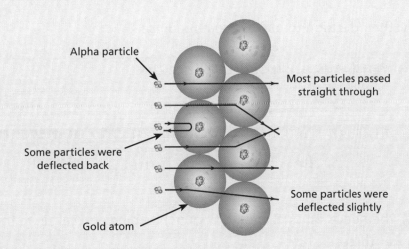

Alpha particle

Most particles passed straight through

Some particles were deflected back

Some particles were deflected slightly

Gold atom

The data from the experiment was used to conclude that:

- atoms were mainly empty space
- atoms had a small positive centre, where most of the mass is found.

Justify the conclusions.   **[6 marks]**

Most of the _____ went straight through the gold foil.

This means they did not hit anything with mass and so the _____

must be mainly empty space.

Some of the alpha particles _____ ,

and some _____ . This must mean they were

_____ by a like charge. But as this only happened

occasionally, we can conclude there is a _____ to

the nucleus and this must be where most of the particles or mass is found

in the atom.

3 · Forces P2 • Grade 4–5 🔒

Some students are investigating how the gradient of a ramp affects the motion of a trolley rolling down it. At each gradient they time the interval between the trolley being released from the top of the ramp and reaching the bottom of the ramp.

At one gradient they record the time intervals as being:

| 8.2 s | 7.9 s | 8.1 s | 10.9 s |

a) Justify their decision to make repeat readings.   **[2 marks]**

Repeat readings are important because ....

.... There might be a

slight pause in releasing the vehicle, an error in measuring

.... or the vehicle might change .... slightly.

b) Justify their decision to eliminate the final reading and calculate the mean of the other three.   **[2 marks]**

The first three readings are .... to each other with

small gaps between, but the .... is significantly different

with a much .... gap.

Taking the .... of the other three will give an answer

nearer to the true value.

Exam practice questions

(25)

1 | Cell Biology P1 • Grade 4–5

This question is about cell structure.

The diagram below shows a cell.

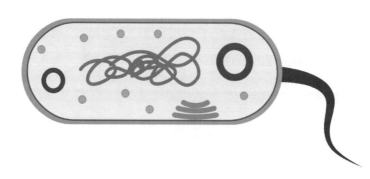

Justify that this cell is a bacterium.   **[4 marks]**

....

....

....

....

....

2 | Inheritance, Variation and Evolution ②• Grade 4–5

This question is about classification of living things.

There are many types of bird that are commonly called a robin.

The picture below shows a native British robin, and its binominal name is *Erithacus rubecula*.

Justify the need for a systematic naming system for all living things.   **[3 marks]**

....

....

....

....

....

3 | Chemical Changes ① • Grade 4–5 ⊖

A student investigated the reaction of magnesium with different types of acid.

This was the method used:

1. 10 cm³ of the same concentration of each acid or pure water was measured and put into separate, labelled test tubes.

2. 0.1 g of magnesium metal was added to each test tube.

3. The reaction was observed.

Here is a diagram of the results.

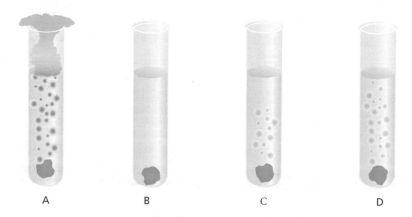

a) Justify that test tube B was the control and contained pure water. **[4 marks]**

....

....

....

....

b) Write the four liquids in order of reactivity with the most reactive first.

Justify your order of reactivity. **[3 marks]**

....

....

....

....

4 **Bonding, Structure, and the Properties of Matter ℗ • Grade 4–5**

This question is about the structure and bonding of substances.

The table shows some information about three different substances.

Substance	Melting point (°C)	Boiling point (°C)	Conductivity when solid (arbitrary units)	Conductivity when in aqueous solution (arbitrary units)
A	114	184	0	Insoluble
B	801	1465	0	80 000
C	1538	2862	99 300	Insoluble

Justify that substance B is an ionic compound. [4 marks]

....

....

....

....

....

5 Energy P1 • Grade 4–5

A company has two designs for an insulated drinks cup.

Design A has an inner and outer layer made of thin recycled plastic with cardboard filling the space between the layers.

Design B has inner and outer layers made from aluminium with a vacuum between them.

Justify the company's decision to put Design B into production rather than Design A. [4 marks]

....

....

....

....

....

....

6 Electricity P1 • Grade 4–5

Some students need to measure the resistance of a component as part of their practical investigation. They could do so by using a power supply to make a current flow through it, measuring the potential difference across the component and the current flow and then dividing the p.d. by the current.

Instead, they decide to use a resistance meter (or ohmmeter) such as this one and measure the resistance directly.

Justify their decision. [3 marks]

....

....

....

....

....

Total score: .... / 25

Mixed Questions

1 Homeostasis P2 • Grade 1–3

The endocrine system helps to co-ordinate and control the body.

a) The diagram shows the glands in the endocrine system.

Name the glands labelled X, Y and Z.　　　　　　　　**[3 marks]**

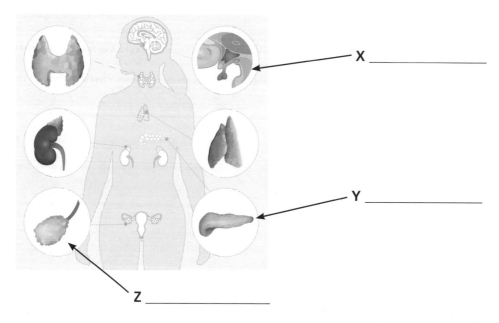

X _____

Y _____

Z _____

b) Write down **two** ways that hormonal responses differ from nervous responses.

....

....

....

2 Inheritance, Variation and Evolution P2 • Grade 1–3

The diagram shows the days of a typical menstrual cycle.

1	5	14	28

a) What process happens on Day 14?　　　　　　　　**[1 mark]**

....

b) Name the hormone that causes the egg to mature in the ovaries. **[1 mark]**

....

c) Progesterone helps to maintain the lining of the womb.

On what day would you expect progesterone to be highest? **[1 mark]**

Tick (✔) **one** box.

Day 1 ☐

Day 5 ☐

Day 14 ☐

Day 21 ☐

3 Bioenergetics ⓟ • Grade 1–3 ☺

This question is about photosynthesis.

a) Name the products of photosynthesis. **[2 marks]**

....

Some students measured the rate of photosynthesis of pond weed at different light intensities.

The graph shows their results.

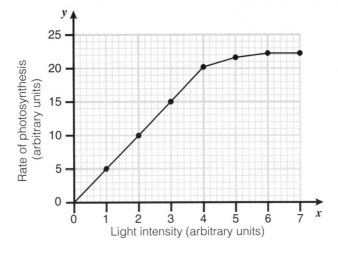

b) What is the rate of photosynthesis at a light intensity of 3.5 arbitrary units? **[1 mark]**

....

c) At what light intensity does the rate of photosynthesis become constant? **[1 mark]**

....

4 Cell Biology P1 • Grade 1–3

The diagram shows a plant cell.

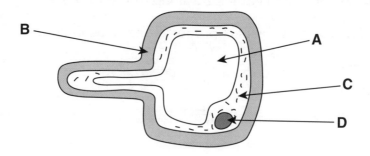

a) Give the name of this cell. [1 mark]

....

b) What is the name of the structure labelled B? [1 mark]

....

c) Which label shows where mitochondria will be found? [1 mark]

....

5 Inheritance, Variation and Evolution P2 • Grade 1–3 🖩

Bacteria can evolve quickly because they reproduce at such a fast rate.

Some bacteria have evolved to become resistant to antibiotics.

MRSA is a bacteria that has evolved to become resistant to the antibiotic methicillin.

The graph shows how the number of cases of MRSA blood infections has changed over seven years.

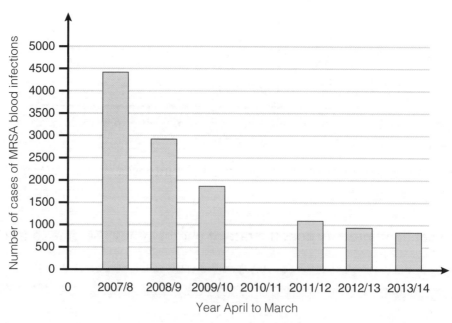

a) In the year 2010/11 there were 1480 cases of MRSA blood infections.

Plot this result on the graph. [1 mark]

b) In hospitals, improved hygiene has reduced the incidence of antibiotic-resistant organisms.

Calculate the percentage decrease in the number of MRSA infections between 2007/8 and 2013/14.

Give your answer to 1 significant figure. **[1 mark]**

....

....

.... %

c) Describe how antibiotic-resistant populations of bacteria develop. **[3 marks]**

....

....

....

....

6 ⬤ **Organisation P1 • Grade 4–5 ▦ ☉**

A student is investigating respiration.

a) Complete the word equation for respiration: **[2 marks]**

oxygen   + ...   ➔   carbon dioxide   + ...

b) A student wants to investigate how his breathing rate changes with exercise of different intensities.

He measures his breathing rate at rest, after walking briskly for two minutes, jogging for two minutes and sprinting for two minutes. He records his results in the table.

Exercise	Breaths per minute
Resting (no exercise)	16
Walking	18
Jogging	25
Sprinting	32

A student plotted these results as a bar chart.

Draw on the chart the result for walking. **[1 mark]**

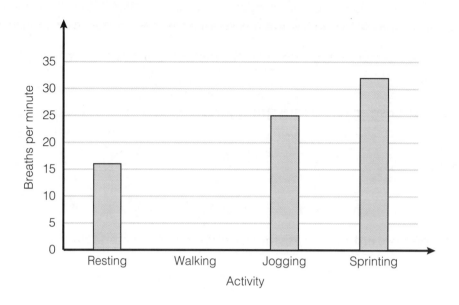

c) Describe how a student's breathing rate changes with intensity of exercise. **[1 mark]**

....

....

7 Infection and Response ⓟ • Grade 4–5 ▦

Measles is a disease caused by a virus.

Children are usually given a vaccination to protect them against measles.

a) Describe how the body responds when a vaccinated person encounters the measles virus.

[4 marks]

....

....

....

....

b) In 2016, there were 531 cases of measles in the UK. 420 of these cases were in people who had not been vaccinated. A number of these cases were linked to music festivals and other large public events.

Calculate the percentage of people who caught measles in 2016 who had not been vaccinated. Give your answer to the nearest whole number. **[2 marks]**

....

....

Percentage = ...

c) How is measles spread? **[1 mark]**

Tick (✔) **one** box.

By air ☐

By direct contact ☐

By water ☐

By insect vector ☐

d) AIDS is a disease that is also caused by a virus.

Give **one** way that the virus causing AIDS is spread. **[1 mark]**

....

e) Explain why it is difficult to treat diseases such as measles and AIDS with drugs. **[3 marks]**

....

....

....

....

8 Inheritance, Variation and Evolution ⑫ • Grade 4–5 ▣

Mendel used the term 'breeding true' in his experiments.

a) What term is used to describe the genotype of an organism that 'breeds true'? **[1 mark]**

....

The table shows some results from one of Mendel's experiments.

Parent plant 1 Breeding true	Parent plant 2 Breeding true	F1 generation	F2 generation	Ratio of offspring in F2 generation
Round seed	Wrinkled seed	Round	5400 round 1820 wrinkled	2.97 : 1
Red flowers	White flowers	Red	700 red 230 white	3.04 : 1
Red	Small plants	Tall	1800 tall 585 small	

The F1 generation are the results obtained when parent 1 and parent 2 are crossed.

The F2 generation are the results when two of the F1 generation are crossed.

b) Calculate the ratio of tall to small plants in the F2 generation.

Give your answer to 2 decimal places. **[1 mark]**

....

c) The diagram shows how the sperm and egg cells are formed in humans by meiosis.

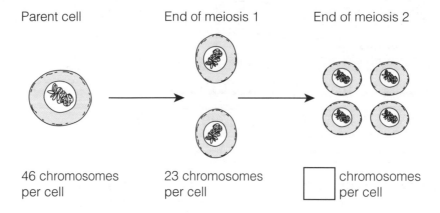

Parent cell   End of meiosis 1   End of meiosis 2

46 chromosomes per cell   23 chromosomes per cell   ☐ chromosomes per cell

Complete the diagram by writing how many chromosomes will be present in each cell at the end of meiosis 2. **[1 mark]**

d) Name the organ where meiosis occurs to produce the male gametes. **[1 mark]**

....

e) If a male gamete carrying an X chromosome fuses with an egg cell, what will be the sex of the offspring? Explain your answer. **[2 marks]**

....

....

f) In asexual reproduction, a different type of cell division is involved.

Name the type of cell division involved in asexual reproduction. **[1 mark]**

....

g) Sexual reproduction in animals requires the fusion of an egg and sperm cell.

Name the two gametes involved in sexual reproduction in plants. **[1 mark]**

....

9 **Using Resources** **P2** • **Grade 1–3**

This question is about the manufacture of clothing.

A manufacturing company produces a LCA for the clothing it produces.

a) What does LCA stand for? **[1 mark]**

....

b) Which **one** of the steps below is not part of the LCA of clothing?   [1 mark]

Tick (✔) **one** box.

The style of the clothing ☐

How much of the clothing can be recycled ☐

The effect on the environment of extracting the raw materials to produce the clothing ☐

The amount of carbon dioxide produced in the manufacture of the clothing ☐

10   Atomic Structure and the Periodic Table P1 • Grade 1–3

A student wanted to separate some pure water from a mixture of ink and water using the equipment shown in the diagram.

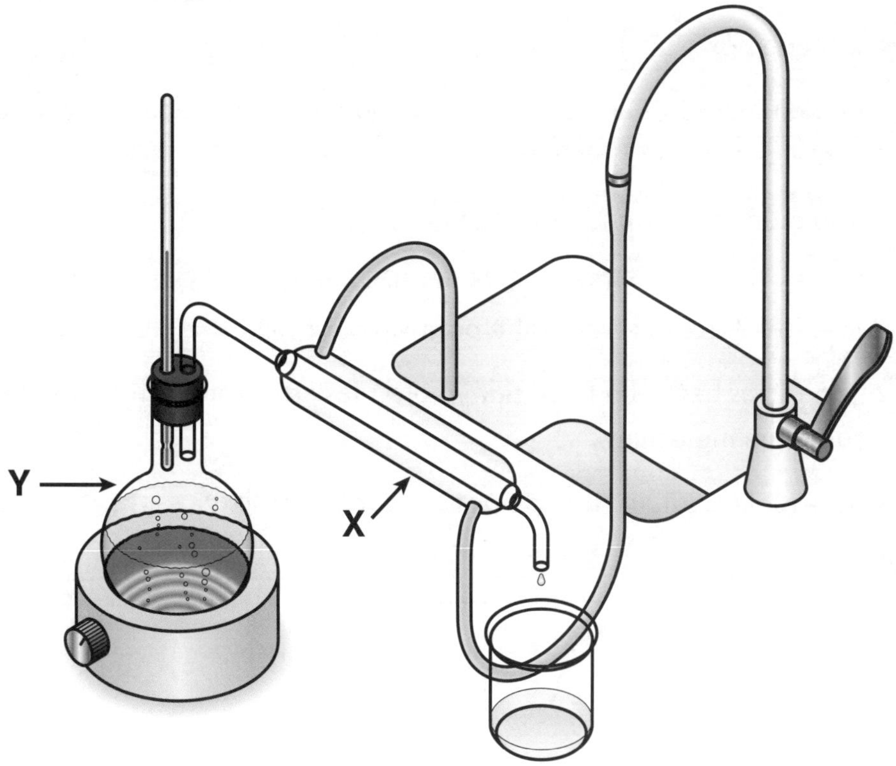

a) Name the pieces of apparatus labelled X and Y.   [2 marks]

X: ....

Y: ....

b) Describe what happens at X and Y in terms of the changes of state.   [2 marks]

At X:

....

....

At Y:

....

....

11 Bonding, Structure, and the Properties of Matter P1 • Grade 1–3

This question is about the alkali metals and their compounds.

The table shows the melting points of some alkali metals.

Element	Melting point in °C
Lithium	181
Sodium	98
Potassium	63
Rubidium	39

a) Why does rubidium have a lower melting point than potassium?   **[1 mark]**

Tick (✔) **one** box.

Rubidium is ionic and contains ionic bonds and potassium is covalent and contains covalent bonds.   ☐

Rubidium is ionic and potassium is metallic.   ☐

The forces between the rubidium ions and the delocalised electrons are weaker than the forces between the potassium ions and the delocalised electrons.   ☐

The forces between potassium molecules are stronger than the forces between rubidium molecules.   ☐

b) Why does solid sodium chloride not conduct electricity?   **[1 mark]**

Tick (✔) **one** box.

It contains a non-metal.   ☐

The ions cannot move.   ☐

It contains a metal.   ☐

It contains ions.   ☐

12 Atomic Structure and the Periodic Table P1 • Grade 1–3

Sodium is a metal in the periodic table:

23
Na
11

a) Identify the number of protons that are present in a sodium atom. **[1 mark]**

Tick (✔) **one** box.

11 ☐

12 ☐

23 ☐

34 ☐

b) Write down the two particles in the nucleus that give an atom its mass. **[2 marks]**

....

....

c) Sodium-24 is an isotope of sodium.

Choose the statement that explains what the term isotope means. **[1 mark]**

Tick (✔) **one** box.

An isotope has a different number of protons. ☐

An isotope has a different number of neutrons. ☐

An isotope has a different number of electrons. ☐

An isotope has a different number of protons and neutrons. ☐

13 Organic Chemistry ℗2 • Grade 4–5

The diagram shows compound A. Compound A is a hydrocarbon.

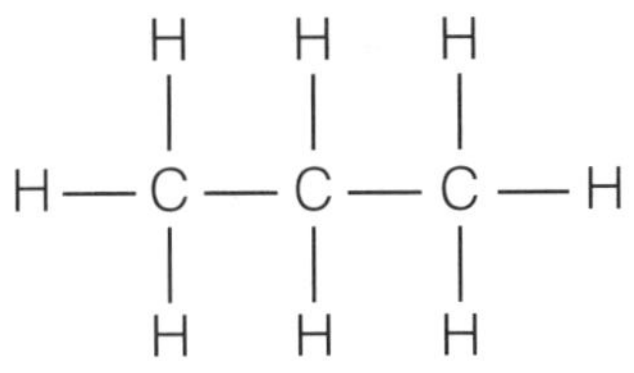

a) What is the molecular formula of compound A? **[1 mark]**

....

b) What is the name of compound A? **[1 mark]**

....

c) Compound A can be burnt as a fuel.

Give the products of the complete combustion of Compound A. **[2 marks]**

....

....

14 Atomic Structure and the Periodic Table P1 • Grade 4–5

An atom of phosphorus has the symbol $^{31}_{15}P$.

a) Give the number of protons, neutrons and electrons in this atom of phosphorus. **[3 marks]**

Number of protons = ...

Number of neutrons = ...

Number of electrons = ...

b) Why is phosphorus in Group 5 of the periodic table? **[1 mark]**

....

15 Using Resources P2 • Grade 4–5

A manufacturing company produces a LCA for the cars it produces.

a) Why is a LCA useful to customers? **[1 mark]**

....

b) Other than the LCA, give one factor that customers might consider when buying a car. **[1 mark]**

....

c) Which of the steps below is part of the LCA of a car? **[1 mark]**

Tick (✔) **one** box.

The top speed of the car ☐

How much of the car can be recycled ☐

The colour of the car ☐

The price of the car to consumers ☐

d) A company is making new shopping bags. Shopping bags can be made from plastic or paper.

Explain the environmental impact of making bags from paper and from plastic. **[4 marks]**

....

....

....

....

....

....

....

An astronaut is on a space walk outside the International Space Station (ISS).

The ISS is moving around the Earth.

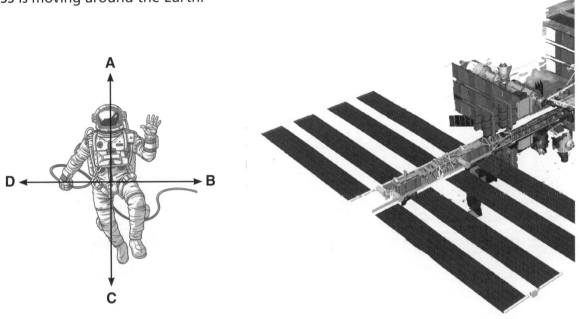

a) In the diagram the astronaut is currently stationary with respect to the ISS.

Choose which of the following statements is correct. **[1 mark]**

Tick (✔) **one** box.

There are no forces acting on the astronaut. ☐

Forces A & D must be the opposite. ☐

Forces B & C must be the same. ☐

Forces A & C and B & D cancel each other out. ☐

b) The astronaut wants to move to the left, away from the ISS.

Identify the force that will need to increase to make the astronaut accelerate to the left.

Tick (✔) **one** box. **[1 mark]**

A ☐

B ☐

C ☐

D ☐

c) The diagram shows the forces acting on the astronaut during part of his space walk.

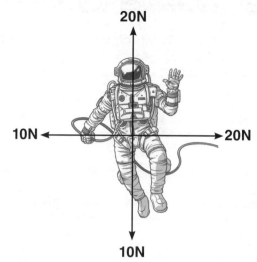

Draw an arrow on the diagram to show the direction the astronaut will travel in.   **[1 mark]**

The graph shows the motion of the astronaut for part of his space walk.

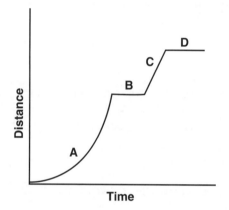

d) Identify the section when the astronaut was accelerating.   **[1 mark]**

Tick (✔) **one** box.

A ☐

B ☐

C ☐

D ☐

e) Identify the section when the astronaut was travelling at a constant speed.   **[1 mark]**

Tick (✔) **one** box.

A ☐

B ☐

C ☐

D ☐

f) The ISS travels a distance of 840 000 metres in 2 minutes.

Calculate the mean speed of the ISS. Use the following equation:

$$\text{mean speed} = \frac{\text{distance}}{\text{time}}$$

[2 marks]

Mean speed = ... m/s

17 Particle Model of Matter ℗ • Grade 1–3 ▣

The UK coast is eroded by sea waves.

The photograph shows the large rocks used in the sea defences.

Each large rock has a mass of 2400 kg and is not moved by the waves.

a) Write down the equation that links density, mass and volume. **[1 mark]**

....

....

b) Basalt is a rock used for sea defences.

A basalt rock has a volume of 0.8 m³.

Calculate the density of basalt. Choose the correct unit from the box. **[3 marks]**

kg m³	m³ / kg	kg / m³

Density = ... Unit: ....

The graph shows how the resistance of a component X varies with light intensity.

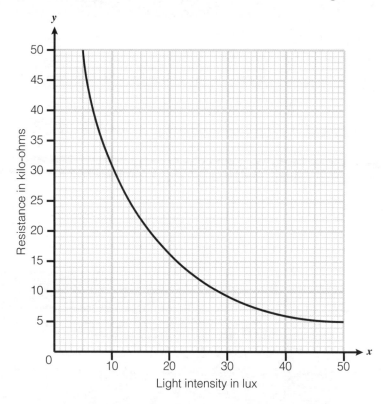

a) Give the name of component X. [1 mark]

....

b) What is the resistance of component X when the light intensity is 35 lux? [1 mark]

....

c) When the light intensity is 35 lux, the current through the circuit is 0.0003 A.

Calculate the reading on the voltmeter when the light intensity is 35 lux. [2 marks]

....

....

....

A heater is used to heat a 1.5 kg metal block.

The table shows how the temperature of the block increased over time.

Time in s	Temperature in °C
0	20.3
60	22.8
120	24.9
180	28.0
240	31.2
300	35.1

The graph shows how temperature changes over time.

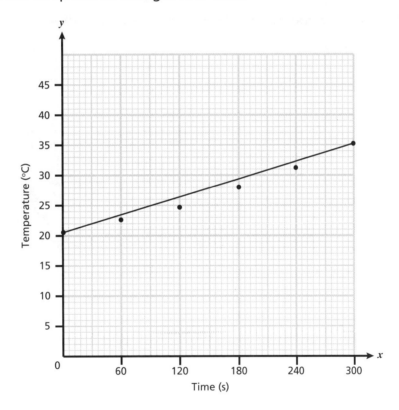

a) Calculate the gradient of the graph. [2 marks]

....

....

....

b) The heater provides thermal energy at a rate of 54 W.

Use the value for the gradient of the graph to calculate the specific heat capacity of the metal block.

Explain how specific heat capacity is related to the change in thermal energy. **[3 marks]**

....

....

....

....

20 Magnetism and Electromagnetism P2 • Grade 4–5

The diagram shows a constant current passing through a straight wire in the downward direction indicated by the arrow.

A magnetic plotting compass is positioned near the wire as shown.

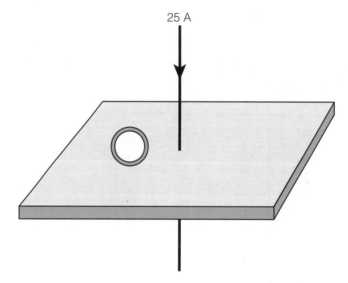

25 A

a) On the diagram, draw an arrow to show the direction the magnetic needle inside the compass is pointing. **[1 mark]**

b) Explain the reason why the needle points in the direction you have shown. **[2 marks]**

....

....

....

c) The diagram shows the Earth, with magnetic South (geographic North) at the top and magnetic North (geographic South) at the bottom.

Draw magnetic field lines on the diagram to show the Earth's magnetic field.   **[2 marks]**

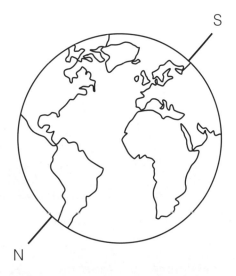

21 Waves ⓟ2 • Grade 4–5 🔢

The diagram shows a wave travelling to the right over a period of 0.5 s.

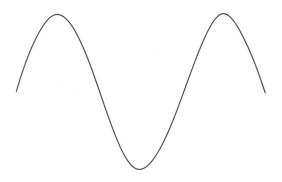

a) What is the frequency of this wave?

Include the unit in your answer.   **[2 marks]**

b) Show the amplitude of the wave on the diagram.   **[1 mark]**

c) If the wave speed is 90 m/s, what is the wavelength?   **[2 marks]**

The photograph shows a scientist monitoring radiation in the environment using a Geiger-Muller tube. They are reading an average of 75 counts per second.

a) Complete the sentences using the words in the box. **[3 marks]**

Alpha	Beta	Gamma	Neutron	Electron	Proton	Omega

Nuclear radiation can be hazardous. .... particles travel short distances

and can be stopped by a sheet of paper. .... particles travel at high

speed. They can be stopped by a sheet of aluminium. .... rays are

electromagnetic radiation from the nucleus.

b) The scientist is wearing protective clothing. Explain why they are wearing protective clothing. **[2 marks]**

....

....

....

....

c) When the scientist returns to the base, they test the Geiger-Muller tube. The reading averages 1 count per second.

Where has the radiation come from that causes the reading of 1 count per second? **[1 mark]**

Tick (✔) **one** box.

The Geiger-Muller tube is faulty. ☐

There is natural background radiation present. ☐

The base is in a radioactive zone. ☐

Their protective clothing is contaminated. ☐

d) Which of the following shows a beta particle? [1 mark]

Tick (✔) **one** box.

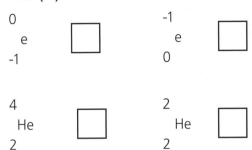

e) The scientist discovers that there is some radon gas present at the site.

Radon undergoes alpha decay to form an isotope of polonium.

Complete the nuclear equation below by adding the missing numbers. [2 marks]

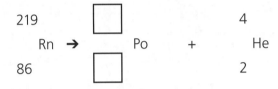

f) The scientist eventually publishes a paper on her findings. Their paper is peer-reviewed before publication.

Suggest why their paper needs to be peer-reviewed. [2 marks]

....

....

Total score: .... / 109

Index of Topics

This grid tells you which questions in this book offer practice for each of the specification topics across the three subjects in Combined Science.

Topic	Page	Question	Example question	Complete the example	Exam practice question
Inheritance, Variation and Evolution, Paper 2	13	6			✓
	14	7			✓
	33	1			✓
	35	7			✓
	42	6			✓
	48	1	✓		
	58	6			✓
	69	7			✓
	69	8			✓
	103	2		✓	
	104	1			✓
	125	2			✓
	134	2			✓
	201	2			✓
	204	2			✓
	206	5			✓
	209	8			✓
Ecology, Paper 2	6	3			✓
	20	1			✓
	35	6			✓
	39	2		✓	
	40	1			✓
	50	4			✓
	59	8			✓
	119	5			✓
	127	5			✓
	128	7			✓
	165	3			✓
	179	3			✓
	179	4			✓
	180	5			✓
CHEMISTRY					
Atomic Structure and the Periodic Table, Paper 1	14	10			✓
	15	11			✓
	19	2		✓	
	20	3			✓
	23	9			✓
	27	3		✓	
	28	2			✓
	31	15			✓
	33	3		✓	
	34	3			✓
	36	9			✓
	38	1	✓		
	52	7			✓
	55	2		✓	
	59	10			✓
	61	12			✓
	69	5			✓
	70	10			✓
	74	2			✓
	77	7			✓
	81	3		✓	
	84	6			✓
	97	2			✓
	97	3			✓

Topic	Page	Question	Example question	Complete the example	Exam practice question
Atomic Structure and the Periodic Table, Paper 1 (cont.)	113	7			✓
	113	8			✓
	126	2			✓
	132	1			✓
	139	1			✓
	139	4			✓
	176	1	✓		
	180	6			✓
	181	7			✓
	185	2		✓	
	186	2			✓
	199	2		✓	
	211	10			✓
	212	12			✓
	214	14			✓
Bonding, Structure, and the Properties of Matter, Paper 1	7	4			✓
	10	1	✓		
	41	4			✓
	44	11			✓
	57	5			✓
	65	3		✓	
	72	1	✓		
	84	6			✓
	91	3			✓
	109	2		✓	
	113	7			✓
	121	10			✓
	121	11			✓
	169	2		✓	
	173	9			✓
	174	10			✓
	202	4			✓
	212	11			✓
Quantitative Chemistry, Paper 1	120	8			✓
	121	9			✓
	135	5			✓
	136	7			✓
Chemical Changes, Paper 1	5	2		✓	
	8	6			✓
	23	8			✓
	30	12			✓
	40	2			✓
	59	9			✓
	60	11			✓
	110	1			✓
	121	9			✓
	130	9			✓
	139	3			✓
	147	3		✓	
	152	6			✓
	185	1			✓
	191	2		✓	
	201	3			✓

Topic	Page	Question	Example question	Complete the example	Exam practice question
Electricity, Paper 1	9	9			✓
	12	3			✓
	26	1	✓		
	29	5			✓
	34	5			✓
	39	3		✓	
	61	13			✓
	63	16			✓
	78	9			✓
	80	1	✓		
	83	4			✓
	85	7			✓
	86	9			✓
	93	7			✓
	93	8			✓
	94	1	✓		
	98	4			✓
	99	6			✓
	103	3		✓	
	109	3		✓	
	115	11			✓
	116	1	✓		
	124	1	✓		
	130	10			✓
	135	3			✓
	137	9			✓
	137	10			✓
	140	1	✓		
	153	8			✓
	156	1			✓
	171	3			✓
	171	4			✓
	183	11			✓
	192	3		✓	
	193	1			✓
	203	6			✓
	218	18			✓
Particle Model of Matter, Paper 1	15	12			✓
	29	8			✓
	41	5			✓
	87	10			✓
	123	17			✓
	142	2		✓	
	145	8			✓
	148	2			✓
	152	7			✓
	158	6			✓
	162	3		✓	
	164	2			✓
	189	7			✓
	217	17			✓
Atomic Structure, Paper 1	19	2		✓	
	53	12			✓
	53	13			✓
	53	14			✓
	69	6			✓

Topic	Page	Question	Example question	Complete the example	Exam practice question
Atomic Structure, Paper 1 (cont.)	71	13			✓
	222	22			✓
Forces, Paper 2	9	8			✓
	15	13			✓
	16	14			✓
	22	6			✓
	25	12			✓
	29	7			✓
	32	1	✓		
	37	11			✓
	49	2		✓	
	55	3		✓	
	71	11			✓
	71	14			✓
	75	3			✓
	89	2		✓	
	99	7			✓
	114	10			✓
	118	3			✓
	122	12			✓
	122	13			✓
	126	3			✓
	133	2		✓	
	136	8			✓
	137	11			✓
	159	7			✓
	179	2			✓
	183	12			✓
	184	1	✓		
	189	8			✓
	197	6			✓
	200	3		✓	
	215	16			✓
Waves, Paper 2	5	3		✓	
	45	14			✓
	47	18			✓
	52	8			✓
	62	14			✓
	71	12			✓
	79	10			✓
	92	6			✓
	119	4			✓
	123	16			✓
	154	1	✓		
	182	9			✓
	221	21			✓
Magnetism and Electro-magnetism, Paper 2	29	6			✓
	62	15			✓
	80	1	✓		
	168	1	✓		
	171	4			✓
	220	20			✓

Notes

Answers

Any extended answer questions in this workbook contain a model full-mark answer. In the exam, extended response questions are marked according to your level of response and there are 2 marks for each level. Examiners will look at the overall quality of the answer.

Pages 4–9: Choose

Complete the example

2. Chemical reactions happen when a new substance is made.
   Oxidation is an example of a chemical reaction where a substance gains **oxygen**.

3. Infrared waves are used in electrical heaters and for cooking.
   Sound waves are longitudinal waves.

Exam practice questions

1. Oestrogen [1]
   Follicle stimulating hormone [1]
   Luteinising hormone [1]
2. cellulose [1]
   amino acids [1]
3. P = photosynthesis [1]
   Q = respiration [1]
   R = combustion [1]
   S = decomposition (*Accept* respiration) [1]
4. A = Solid [1]
   B = Liquid [1]
   C = Gas [1]
5. chlorine [1]
   hydrogen [1]
6. increase [1]
   limiting [1]
   excess [1]
   evaporating [1]
7. A = nitrogen [1]
   B = oxygen [1]
   C = carbon dioxide (*Accept* water) [1]
8. 7750 N [1]
9. resistance of [1]
10. kinetic [1]

Pages 10-17: Give

Complete the example

2. **b)** Right ventricle
   c) Pulmonary vein
3. **1** The base of the stand should be **clamped** so that it can't **topple over when weights are added**.
   2 The total weight should be **limited** so that **the risk from it falling is restricted**.

Exam practice questions

1. **a)** Insulin (*Accept* glucagon) [1]
   b) Pancreas [1]
2. **a)** Oxygen [1]
   b) Carbon dioxide [1]
   c) Acid rain [1]
3. *In any order:* diameter; length; material [3]
4. By becoming infected with the disease [1]
5. **a)** Malignant [1]
   b) Genes/genetic factors [1]
6. **a)** *Any three of:* geographical changes; new predators; new diseases; more competitors; catastrophic events; human actions [3]
   b) *Any suitable answer,* e.g. Dodo, mammoth, sabre-toothed tiger [1]
7. **a)** B [1]
   b) The Ostracoderm lived longer ago. [1]
      Fossils that are lower down are older. [1]
8. *Any two of:* coal; oil; gas; nuclear [2]
9. **a)** C_nH_{2n+2} [1]
   b) C_4H_{10} [1]
10. Protons 11; Electrons 11 [1]
    Neutrons 13 [1]
11. **a)** Halogens [1]
    b) Cl_2 [1]
    c) K^+ (*Accept* K^{1+} *and* K^{+1}) [1]
       Br^- (*Accept* Br^{1-} *and* Br^{-1}) [1]
12. *In any order:* length; breadth / width; height; mass [4]
13. **a)** *Any three from:* tiredness; exhaustion; being distracted; under the influence of drugs; being drunk; poor visibility; age; genetics; practice/experience. [3]
    b) *Any three from:* vehicle overloaded; tyres with poor tread; brakes in poor condition; water on roads; icy conditions. [3]
14. The change in speed [1]
    The change in direction [1]
    The weight/mass of the vehicle [1]
15. **a)** *Any two of:* wind turbines; solar panels; waves; tides; geothermal [2]
    b) *Advantage – any one from:* reliable; high output; no greenhouse gases produced; large available fuel supply [1]
       Disadvantage – any one from: radioactive waste; expensive to build and decommission; risk of nuclear accident [1]

Pages 18-25: Identify

Complete the example

2. b) E

3. c) Gamma d) Lead

Exam practice questions

1. a) Grass [1]
   b) Stoat [1]
2. The stimulus is the hot plate. [1]
   The receptor is the nerve endings. [1]
   The effector is the muscles in the arm. [1]
3. a) A = Neutron [1]
   B = Electron [1]
   C = Proton [1]
   b) Positive [1]
4. a) thermometer [1]
   b) polystyrene cup [1]
   c) (using the) stirrer [1]
5. *In any order:* B; E; F [2]
6. Mass; Velocity [2]
7. a) A [1]
   b) A and D [2]
   c) B [1]
8. a) Oxygen / O_2 [1]
   b) Oxidation [1]
9. It floats on water. [1]
10. a) Concentration of hydrochloric acid [1]
   b) Time (taken for cross to disappear) [1]
11. a) Volume of gas [1]
   b) *Accept one from:* concentration of hydrogen peroxide; volume of hydrogen peroxide; temperature of reaction mixture [1]

12.

[3]

Pages 26-31: Name

Complete the example

2. b) Xylem cell
   c) Phloem cell
3. a) Sodium **chloride**
   b) Lithium and **bromine**

Exam practice questions

1. a) Platelets [1]
   b) White blood cells (*Accept* phagocytes) [1]
2. a) Proton [1]
   b) Neutron [1]
   c) (Niels) Bohr
3. Single covalent [1]

4. a) *Any one of:* coal; oil, gas; peat. [1]
   b) *Any one of:* wind; solar; geothermal; tidal; biofuel; hydroelectricity; waves. [1]
5. LDR / light dependent resistor [1]
6. Infrared [1]
7. Newton [1]
8. Geiger tube / G–M tube [1]
9. Rose black spot – fungus [1]
   Malaria – protist [1]
   Measles – virus [1]
10. a) Digitalis [1]
   b) Willow [1]
   c) Alexander Fleming [1]
11. a) Pituitary gland [1]
   b) Progesterone, LH and oestrogen [3]
12. a) Bromine [1]
   b) Lead [1]
13. a) Methane / CH_4 [1]
   b) Combustion [1]
   c) Carbon dioxide / CO_2 [1]
14. *In any order:* Carbon dioxide; Methane [2]
15. X = Electron [1]

Pages 32-37: Write

Complete the example

2. a) Glucose ➔ **Ethanol + Carbon dioxide**
   b) Bread *and one from:* beer; wine; cider
3. chlorine + **potassium bromide** ➔ **potassium chloride + bromine**

Exam practice questions

1. Bobcat; Ocelot [2]
2. carbon dioxide + water ➔ glucose + oxygen [1]
3. Sodium + Oxygen ➔ Sodium Oxide [2]
4. CO_2 [1]
5. *In any order:* power supply / battery / cell; lamp; wires. [3]
6. a) Primary consumers [1]
   b) Apex consumers/predators [1]
   c) Secondary consumers [1]

7.

Controlled by their genes	Caused by the environment	Controlled by their genes and caused by the environment
Tom and Jake have brown eyes [1]	Jake has a scar [1]	Tom is 160 cm tall [1] Jake's body mass is 60 kg [1]

8. Methane + Oxygen ➔ Carbon dioxide + water [2]
9. 2, 8, 8, 1 [1]
10. GPE = mass × gravitational field strength × vertical height (GPE = m × g × h) [1]
11. Speed = distance ÷ time [1]

12. *In any order:* mass of the solid; specific latent heat of the solid. **[2]**

Pages 38-47: Complete

Complete the example

2. Peat bogs are often destroyed to provide peat for gardening.

The variety of different species that live there is called the **biodiversity** and this is being reduced.

When the peat decays, it releases **carbon dioxide** into the atmosphere. This can trap heat energy and cause **global warming**.

3. **A** Power station

B Step up transformer

C Step down transformer

D Consumer

Exam practice questions

1. *Labels completed from left to right:*

Precipitation **[1]**

Transpiration **[1]**

Evaporation **[1]**

2. tin oxide + carbon ➔ tin + carbon dioxide **[2]**

3. carbon dioxide + water ➔ glucose + oxygen **[2]**

4.

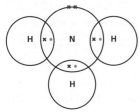

(1 mark for each correct covalent bond; 1 mark for lone pair of electrons on the nitrogen) **[3]**

5. **A** Eureka can **[1]**

B Irregular solid **[1]**

C Measuring cylinder **[1]**

6. trachea **[1]**

bronchioles **[1]**

alveoli **[1]**

gas(eous) **[1]**

7.

Hormone	Site of production	Function
insulin	pancreas	**controls blood glucose levels [1]**
testosterone	**testes [1]**	controls production of secondary sexual characteristics

8. *Labels completed clockwise from top left:*

Vena cava **[1]**

Aorta **[1]**

Left atrium **[1]**

Right ventricle **[1]**

9. increases **[1]**

water; partially **[2]**

0.5 **[1]**

10 surroundings **[1]**

decrease / get lower / fall **[1]**

exothermic reactions / exothermic changes / exothermic chemical reactions / exothermic chemical changes. **[1]**

11.

(1 mark for correct charge on magnesium ion; 1 mark for no electrons in the outer shell of magnesium ion; 1 mark for correct charge on oxide ion; 1 mark for eight electrons in the outer shell of oxide ion) **[4]**

12. a) magnesium + hydrochloric acid ➔ magnesium chloride + hydrogen

(1 mark for each in either order) **[2]**

b) The independent variable is concentration (of hydrochloric acid). **[1]**

The dependent variable is mass. **[1]**

13. CO_2 (g) + $Ca(OH)_2$ (aq) ➔ $CaCO_3$ (s) + H_2O (l) **[4]**

14. a) visible light **[1]**

b) radio waves **[1]**

c) ultraviolet **[1]**

d) microwaves **[1]**

e) X-rays (*Accept* gamma rays) **[1]**

f) infrared **[1]**

g) gamma rays (*Accept* X-rays) **[1]**

15. a) Gravitational potential **[1]**

b) Gravitational potential **[1]**

c) Elastic potential **[1]**

16. A liquid **[1]**

B mixture of solid and liquid **[1]**

C solid **[1]**

17. a) A: 40 **[1]**

b) B: 10.5 **[1]**

18. A = Lamp/strobe light **[1]**

B = Dipper/wave generator **[1]**

C = Shallow tray of water **[1]**

Pages 48-53: Define

Complete the example

2. The rate **at which distance is travelled**.

3. a) A single **element / compound / substance**.

(You could also say 'not mixed with any other substance')

b) A substance that has had **nothing added to it**.

(You could also just say 'unadulterated')

Exam practice questions

1. Osmosis is the movement of water from a dilute solution **[1]** to a concentrated solution through a partially permeable membrane. **[1]**

2. Total amount of greenhouse gases / carbon dioxide emitted [1]
   over the full life cycle of a product, service or event. [1]
3. a) Transpiration is loss of water from the aerial parts / leaves of a plant. [2]
   b) Translocation is the movement of dissolved sugars through the phloem tissue in a plant. [2]
4. a) All the living organisms / biotic factors and all the non-living / abiotic factors in an area / habitat. [1]
   b) All the organisms / populations living in a habitat. [1]
5. a) Transfers energy to the surroundings [1]
      so the temperature of the surroundings increases. [1]
   b) The minimum amount of energy that particles must have to react. [1]
6. Water that is safe to drink. [1]
7. a) The smallest part of an element that can exist. [1]
   b) An atom that has gained electrons [1]
      or lost electrons. [1]
8. The rate at which a wave passes a fixed point (*Accept* number of waves passing a point in a second). [1]
9. Energy which is stored in an object due to it being in motion. [1]
10. Energy which is stored in a flexible object due to it being stretched, compressed, twisted or bent. [1]
11. The amount of energy needed to increase the temperature of one kilogram of a material by one degree C. [1]
12. The amount of time for the level of activity of a particular sample to drop to half its level. [1]
13. The adding of radioactive substances to an object. [1]
14. The process by which an object is exposed to ionising radiation. [1]

Pages 54-63: Describe

Complete the example

2. The atom is a ball of **positive** charge with **negative electrons** embedded in it.
3. The graph shows the relationship between distance and **time**. On a graph like this if the line is horizontal it means that the object is **stationary**. If the line has a positive gradient it means that the object is **moving away from the starting point**.
   In this graph the object starts off by travelling at a **steady speed** and then **stops**. It then moves at a greater **steady speed**, then **stops** and finally **returns to the starting point**.

Exam practice questions

1. Digested by amylase. [1]
   Turned into sugars. [1]
2. *Description should include any four points from:* Increases blood pressure; Increases the risk of cardiovascular disease / heart attacks; Increases the risk of strokes; Causes lung cancer; Can lead to bronchitis or emphysema. [4]

3. Filter the mixture. [1]
   Collect the sand / solid / residue in the filter paper. [1]
   Dry the residue by patting dry with absorbent paper / putting in a drying oven / drying with a hairdryer. [1]
4. The food colouring is a mixture / formulation. [1]
   It is made of three different colours. [1]
5. *Description should include any four points from:* sodium (atom) loses an electron; chlorine (atom) gains an electron; chloride ion formed; chloride has negative charge / is a negative ion / particle; sodium ion formed; sodium has positive charge; oppositely charged ions attract; a giant structure / lattice is formed. [4]
6. From parts of organisms that have not decayed. [1]
   Because the conditions needed for decay are absent. [1]
   Parts of the organism are replaced by minerals. [1]
   As preserved footprints / burrows / rootlet traces / bones / teeth. [1]
7. As the percentage of oxygen increases, the breathing rate decreases. [1]
   At higher levels, the breathing rate levels off. [1]
   Minimum breathing rate is about 14.5 breaths per minute. [1]
8. Place quadrat randomly / description of how randomness is achieved or systematically / description of how systematic placement is achieved. [1]
   Count and record number of buttercups in quadrat.
   Repeat (more than 5 times) for different locations. [1]
   Calculate a mean number of buttercups per quadrat. [1]
   Measure the area of the ecosystem. Estimate the buttercup population using the area of the quadrat. [1]
9. a) The student would see bubbles / hear fizzing / observe effervescence [1]
      and the zinc would get smaller / disappear. [1]
   b) Use a burning splint. [1]
      If the gas is hydrogen, you will hear a (squeaky) pop. [1]
10. a) In order of their atomic masses. [1]
    b) Mendeleev left gaps for elements that he thought had not been discovered. [1]
       Mendeleev changed the order based on atomic masses / ordered the elements by their chemical reactions. [1]
    c) No gaps [1]
       Group 0 / Noble gases discovered. [1]
       Elements listed by increasing atomic number. [1]
11. Chlorine: damp litmus paper [1]
    bleached / turns white [1]
    Hydrogen: a burning splint [1]
    pop sound [1]
    Oxygen: glowing splint [1]
    relights [1]
12. The Thorium atom has 2 fewer protons than the Uranium atom. [1]
    The Thorium atom has 2 fewer neutrons than the Uranium atom. [1]

13. *In any order, any three from (2 marks each):* plastic case which acts as an insulator; earth wire which conducts current away if the case becomes live; fuse which blows/melts if excess current flows; cable grip which stops cable being pulled out. **[6]**

14. Transverse: Shake the slinky from side to side or up and down to make transverse waves. **[1]**

Hand movement up and down

Direction of wave movement **[1]**

Longitudinal: Push the slinky backwards and forwards to make longitudinal waves. **[1]**

Hand movement in and out

Compression Expansion

Direction of wave movement

[1]

15 a) Strong **[1]**
and uniform **[1]**
  b) Like a bar magnet / Strongest at the ends of the coil **[1]**

16. Pass a direct current **[1]**
through a conducting wire **[1]**
a magnetic field is produced around the wire/circular magnetic force field is produced around the wire **[1]**
This can be visualised by plotting compasses/iron filings **[1]**

Pages 64-71: Why / What / Which…

Complete the example

2. Length when loaded **minus original length**
3. a) Mixture
Formulation
  b) In pure metals, the layers of **atoms / ions** easily **slide** over each other, but in alloys, the different sizes of **atoms / ions** distort the layers so they can't **slide** as easily.

Exam practice questions

1. aspirin **[1]**
2. a) nucleus **[1]**
  b) DNA **[1]**
  c) *Correct order* – 2, 4, 3, 1
    2 before 4 **[1]**
    4 before 3 **[1]**
    3 before 1 **[1]**
3. a) Water that is safe to drink **[1]**
  b) Chlorine **[1]**

c) *Any two from:* To kill microorganisms; To prevent waterborne disease; To stop people from getting sick or ill. **[2]**
4. a) Independent **[1]**
  b) Control **[1]**
  c) Dependent **[1]**
5. a) Chadwick **[1]**
  b) In the nucleus of most atoms **[1]**
6. Beta radiation (*Accept* high energy electron) **[1]**
Alpha radiation (*Accept* helium nuclei / helium 2+ ion) **[1]**
7. Genome **[1]**
8. Four genetically different cells are produced. **[1]**
9. a) Act as a heat shield / Stop the water in the beaker heating up. **[1]**
  b) Rate of photosynthesis / Number of bubbles given off in a certain time. **[1]**
10. Each isotope has a different number of neutrons. **[1]**
11. Speed is a scalar quantity and only has magnitude. **[1]**
Velocity is a vector quantity and has direction as well as magnitude. **[1]**
12. The effectiveness of the transfer depends upon the colour of the radiator. **[1]**
Matt black is the colour that is most effective at radiating energy. **[1]**
13. Alpha **[1]**
14. a) The object is stationary. **[1]**
  b) The object is travelling at a constant velocity. **[1]**

Pages 72-79: Use

Complete the example

2. This method does not use **expensive / complicated** equipment.
It is also very easy, so that people do not need a lot of **training / experience / knowledge** to be able to administer the vaccine.
3. a) The purpose is to produce **light** so any other outputs are not useful. The **thermal** output is not useful and is **3.2 J**.
  b) Efficiency = (Useful energy transferred out ÷ Total energy supplied) × 100
    = **0.8 ÷ 4** × 100
    = **20%**

Exam practice questions

1. a) *Any one from*: Nitrogen; N_2 **[1]**
  b) *Any one from:* Noble gases; Group 0 **[1]**
  c) $\frac{1}{5}$ **[1]**
2. a) *Any one from:* Fluorine; Chlorine (*Accept F, F_2, Cl, Cl_2*) **[1]**
  b) As you go down the group, melting point increases. (*Accept:* as you go up the group, melting point decreases.) **[1]**
  c) Iodine **[1]**

3. weight = 0.2 x 9.8   [1]
    = 1.96 N   [1]
4. 20 = size of image ÷ 0.06   [1]
    20 x 0.06   [1]
    = 1.2 mm   [1]
5. D   [1]
    Release of toxins in the body cause fever.   [1]
6. *Accept any value from 980–999*   [1]
7. Nucleus   [1]
8. a) 20 : 2   [1]
      = 10 : 1   [1]
  b) There are 55 atoms.   [1]
      There are 47 copper atoms.   [1]
      $\frac{47}{55} \times 100 = 85.454\ 545\ 45$ [1]
      85.5%   [1]

9.

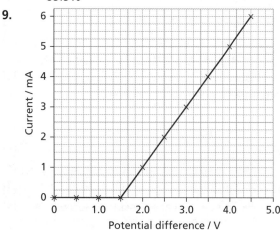

(2 marks for axes labelled correctly; 1 mark for all points plotted correctly; 1 mark for line of best fit)   **[4]**

10. a) 0.5 Hz   [1]
   b) period = 1 ÷ frequency   [1]
       = 1 ÷ 0.5   [1]
       = 2 s   [1]
       If frequency of 10 is used, then alternative answer would be:
       period = 1 ÷ frequency   [1]
       = 1 ÷ 10   [1]
       = 0.1 s   [1]

Pages 80-87 : Draw

Complete the example

2.

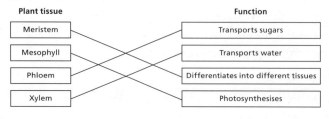

3.

Exam practice questions

1. *Drawing of white blood cell starting to surround and engulf bacterium.*   **[1]**
    Drawing of bacterium shown in a vesicle inside white blood cell   **[1]**
2. Methane – Climate change
    Sulfur dioxide – Acid rain
    Particulates –Global dimming
    (All correct with no additional lines drawn; 1 mark for one or two correct)   **[2]**
3. Hydrogen – Burning splint and hear a pop sound
    Carbon dioxide – Limewater turns milky
    Oxygen – Glowing splint relights
    Chlorine – Damp litmus paper turns white
    (All correct with no additional lines drawn; 2 marks for two or three correct; 1 mark for one correct)   **[3]**
4. *Circuit with correctly connected battery*   **[1]**
    ammeter   **[1]**
    and voltmeter   **[1]**

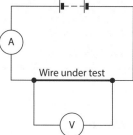

5. *Diagram drawn the same shape with clear lines and no shading.*   **[1]**
    Any two from: the cell membrane; cytoplasm; nucleus *should be labelled.*   **[2]**
6. a)

    (1 mark for 9 electrons in total; 1 mark for two electrons in the first shell and seven electrons in the outer shell)   **[2]**
   b)

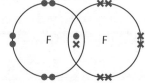

          [2]

7. a) *See diagram* **[1]**
   b) *See diagram* **[1]**

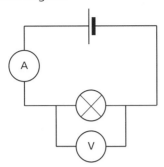

8. *(1 mark for block; 1 mark for heater; 1 mark for thermometer; 1 mark for meters: ammeter in series and voltmeter in parallel.)* **[4]**

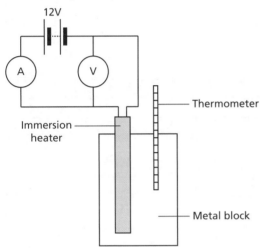

9. *(1 mark for ammeter; 1 mark for voltmeter; 1 mark for ruler; 1 mark for wire.)* **[4]**

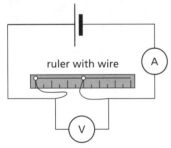

10. *10 circles all drawn in a random arrangement, no particles touching.* **[1]**

Pages 88-93: Sketch

Complete the example

2.

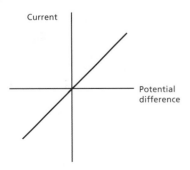

(1 mark for line going through the origin; 1 mark for positive gradient and straight line)

Exam practice questions

1.

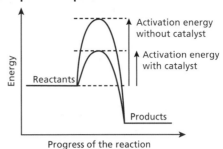

(1 mark for arrow going downwards; 1 mark for labels) **[2]**

2.

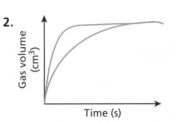

(1 mark for line starting at origin; 1 mark for steeper curve; 1 mark for lines finishing at the same height) **[3]**

3.

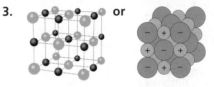

(1 mark for attempt to show 3D; 1 mark for at least 5 sodium ions and 5 chloride ions; 1 mark for a repeating pattern where the chloride is surrounded / connected by 4 sodium ions and each sodium is surrounded / connected to chloride ions.) **[3]**

4.

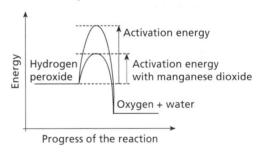

(1 mark for same shape as the current activation energy but lower peak) **[1]**

5.

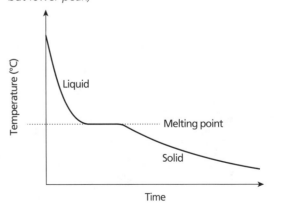

Curved line labelled liquid **[1]**
Horizontal line labelled melting point **[1]**
Curved line labelled solid **[1]**

6.

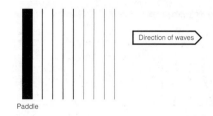

(Four waves drawn; each the same distance apart as the original 4 waves) **[2]**

7.

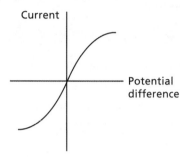

(1 mark for line going through the origin; 1 mark for 's' shape curve.) **[2]**

8.

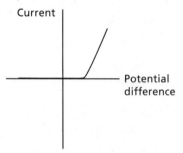

(1 mark for the first part of the graph to the horizontal line on the x-axis, showing where the resistance is very high; 1 mark for a positive gradient straight line.) **[2]**

Pages 94-101: Label

Complete the example

2. a) *See label below. (Accept Bunsen burner)*

   b) *See label below. (Accept condenser)*

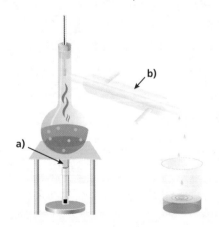

3.

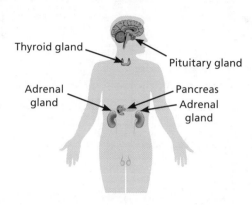

Only one adrenal gland needs to be labelled.

Exam practice questions

1. *Labels as follows from top to bottom:*
   Cell wall **[1]**
   Nucleus **[1]**
   Chloroplast **[1]**
   Vacuole **[1]**
   Cytoplasm **[1]**

2. 23 = Mass number
   11 = Atomic number **[1]**

3.

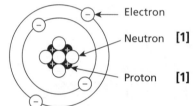

(1 mark for 'proton' correctly labelled; 1 mark for 'neutron' correctly labelled)

4.

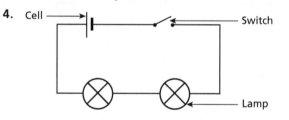

[3]

5.

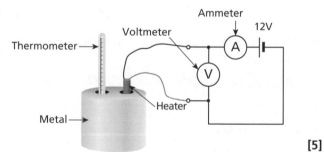

[5]

6.

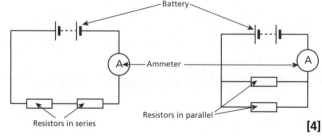

[4]

7.

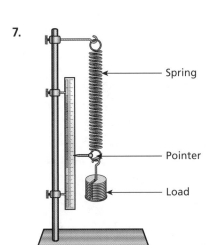

Spring

Pointer

Load

8.

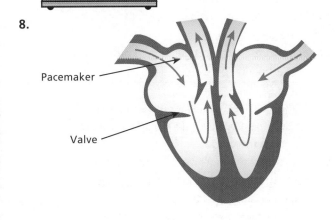

Pacemaker

Valve

9. R = first, second or third cell from the left **[1]**
S = fourth cell from the left **[1]**
T = third cell from the left **[1]**

10.

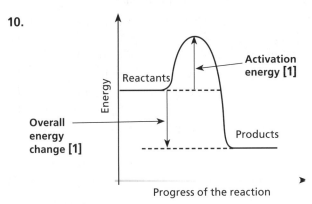

Overall energy change **[1]**

Reactants

Activation energy **[1]**

Products

Progress of the reaction

11. a) *See label below.*
b) *See label below.*

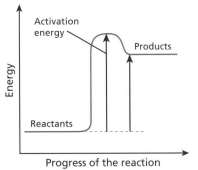

Activation energy

Products

Reactants

Progress of the reaction

[2]

Pages 102-107: Suggest

Complete the example

2. A plant may have sexually reproduced and released **seeds**. These were carried to the area and germinated to produce a plant.
This plant must then have used **asexual** reproduction many times as all the plants in the area are **genetically** identical.

3. a) The lamps are the same design but may **vary** slightly in manufacture or have been treated **differently**. This may result in one of them having a slightly **higher** resistance and therefore being slightly **brighter**.

b) If a fourth lamp is added, the potential difference will be **shared** between four lamps instead of **three**. This means there will be less **potential difference** across each lamp and they will all be **dimmer** than before.

Exam practice questions

1. a) The new potato tubers could separate from the parent plant. **[1]**
Each one could produce shoots and grow into a new plant. **[1]**

b) *Any two from:* taste; resistance to disease; resistance to frosts; rapid growth **[2]**

2. a) Too soft **[1]**

b) As an alloy (with silver, copper and zinc) (*Accept* formulation / mixture with other metals) **[1]**

3. Solar panels won't necessarily provide energy at the time it is most needed / not sunny all the time. **[1]**
Installing a battery will enable some energy to be stored to be used when needed / stored energy can be used at night. **[1]**

4. If they remove the thermometer from the water it will take the temperature of the air which is unlikely to be the same. **[1]**

5. *Any two from:* Seal numbers might drop as they have less food; Seaweed or phytoplankton might increase as less is eaten; Winkle numbers might increase as there is more seaweed for them to eat; Lobster populations could decrease as seals switch to eating more of them to make up for lack of fish; Gull numbers might drop as there will be more competition with the seals for the lobsters; Sea urchin, winkle and limpet numbers might rise as there is more phytoplankton for them to eat. **[2]**

6. a) The pancreas extract contained insulin. **[1]**
The insulin controlled the blood glucose level. **[1]**
However, the injected insulin only lasted for a certain time in the body. **[1]**

b) For: allowed the discovery of insulin / led to treatment for diabetes / saved lives. **[1]**
Against: ethically wrong to harm animals / dogs may respond differently to humans. **[1]**

7. Measuring the mass loss as the reaction happens. [1]
   Measuring the volume of gas produced during the reaction. [1]

8. Distillation [1]
   Reverse osmosis [1]

9. a) The energy supplied will vary according to the amount of sunlight that day. [1]
   b) At some times of year the days are shorter, so less sunlight will be received. [1]
   c) It means energy not being used at that time can be stored [1]
   and used later on when it is needed. [1]

Pages 108–115: Explain

Complete the example

2. Carbon nanotubes contain **delocalised electrons**, which **are free to move through the structure and carry the charge.**

3. If lamps are connected in series, the potential difference supplied by the **cell / battery / power pack** will be divided between the lamps so if there are more lamps then each of the lamps receives **less** and therefore **becomes dimmer**.
   However, if the lamps are connected in parallel, each of the lamps receives **the whole potential difference**. This means that if more lamps are connected then all of them will receive **the full potential difference** and therefore **be bright**.

Exam practice questions

1. Oxygen is added to the metal. [1]
2. To reduce unwanted energy transfer / increase efficiency [1]
   To reduce friction [1]
3. Rowers use muscle contraction in their legs and their arms when rowing but runners mainly use their legs. [1]
   During this contraction, more energy is required which is released from respiration, which happens in mitochondria. [1]
   Therefore rowers need more mitochondria in both their arms and legs. [1]
4. *Explanation should include any four of these points:*
   Many subcellular structures are too small to be seen with a light microscope; Compared to light microscopes, electron microscopes can see smaller specimens because they have; a greater magnification; a higher resolution; greater resolving power; Transmission electron microscopes (TEM) show structures in cells. [4]
5. a) Acts as a control. [1]
   To show that the water is lost from the plants. [1]
   b) B loses much less water than C. [1]

The stomata are mainly on the under surface of the leaf [1]
so in B they are blocked. [1]

6. a) The number of people needing transplants is higher than the number of transplants being carried out. [1]
   The gap between the two is increasing. [1]
   b) *Any two from:* The number of transplants is higher than the number of dead donors; Therefore, each donor must be donating more than one organ; Some organ donations are from live donors, e.g. kidneys. [2]

7. a) Metal atoms lose (outer shell) electrons [1]
   to become positive ions. [1]
   b) Non-metal atoms gain (outer shell) electrons [1]
   to become negative ions. [1]

8. a) *Four from:* The atoms get larger / atomic radii increase;
   Less attraction between the (positive) nucleus and (outer shell) electrons;
   Outer shell electrons are more easily lost;
   To become a positive / 1+ ion; More reactive as you go down the group. [4]
   b) The atoms get larger / Atomic radii increase. [1]
   Less attraction from the (positive) nucleus to attract / gain an electron [1]
   Less reactive as you go down the group [1]
   to become a negative/1– ion as less easily forms chemical bonds. [1]
   c) Atoms have a stable arrangement of electrons.
   (*Accept* full outer shell (of electrons)) [1]

9. a) Particles have more kinetic energy. [1]
   More collisions in the same time. [1]
   More collisions have higher energy / More collisions occur or exceed the activation energy. [1]
   More successful collisions in the same time. [1]
   b) Powder has more surface area than ribbon. [1]
   More particles exposed for collision at the same time. [1]
   More successful collisions in the same amount of time. [1]

10. *Any two from:* The steady speed in a straight line results from a zero resultant force; This doesn't mean that there are no forces acting, but they all cancel each other out; There is a forwards force due to the engine, cancelled out by the opposing forces of friction and air resistance; The balancing of these causes the resultant to be zero. [2]

11. Current is the same in every single component in the circuit / one path for the current to flow / series circuit [1]
    The more resistors there are, the harder it is for current to flow / the fewer resistors there are, the easier it is for current to flow [1]
    Overall resistance is increased when more resistors are added / overall resistance decreases when fewer resistors are added. [1]

Pages 116-123 : Show

Complete the example

2. Hydrogen + Nitrogen $\rightleftharpoons$ Ammonia.

3. Therapeutic ratio for drug **A** is **10**, for drug **B** it is **5** and for drug **C** it is **8**.

Therefore, taking drug **A** would be safest, as it has the **highest** ratio so people would be less likely to take a dangerous dose.

Exam practice questions

1. ammonium chloride $\rightleftharpoons$ ammonia + hydrogen chloride **[1]**

2. 20% oxygen **[1]**

80 : 20 **[1]**

= 8 : 2 = 4 : 1 **[1]**

3. W = m × g

= 20 × 10 **[1]**

= 200 N **[1]**

4. *Correct labels showing amplitude* **[1]**

and wavelength **[1]**

(Accept an arrow for amplitude from the midpoint to the maximum negative displacement and any arrow for wavelength beginning and ending at an equivalent position of the repeating wave.)

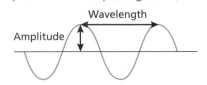

5. % efficiency = $\frac{20}{100}$ × 100 **[1]**

= 20% so twice as efficient **[1]**

6. 6 become pregnant out of a total of 25 **[1]**

So percentage is $\frac{6}{25}$ × 100 = 24% **[1]**

7. Minimum percentage with high blood pressure is

33% + 3% **[1]**

So $\frac{36}{100}$ × 1 000 000 = 360 000 **[1]**

8. Percentage yield =

$\frac{\text{mass of actual product made}}{\text{maximum theoretical yield of product}}$ × 100 **[1]**

= ($\frac{15.8}{63.5}$) × 100 **[1]**

= **24.881 189**, which rounds to 25% **[1]**

9. 125 – 81 = mass of carbon dioxide **[1]**

= 44 g **[1]**

10. Ca^{2+} and O^{2-} **[1]**

11.

Substance	Melting temperature (°C)	Boiling temperature (°C)	State	
X	–7	49	Liquid	**[1]**
Y	1256	1879	Solid	**[1]**
Z	–180	–160	Gas	**[1]**

12. W = m × g **[1]**

so g = W ÷ m = 4.25 ÷ 2.5 **[1]**

= 1.7 N/kg **[1]**

13. Acceleration = change in velocity ÷ time **[1]**

a = (4 − 0) ÷ 0.4 **[1]**

= 10 m/s² **[1]**

14. F = k × e **[1]**

so e = F ÷ k. For spring A 2.5 ÷ 1,000 = 0.0025 m (or 2.5 mm). **[1]**

For spring B 2.5 ÷ 500 = 0.005 m (or 5 mm). **[1]**

Therefore, B extends twice as far as A. **[1]**

15. Useful output = 125 J and energy supplied = 500 J,

so efficiency = 125 ÷ 500 **[2]**

= 25 % **[1]**

16. V = f × λ **[1]**

so λ = v ÷ f = 330 ÷ 256 **[2]**

= 1.289 m or 1289 mm **[1]**

17. Density = mass ÷ volume **[1]**

Volume = l × b × h = 0.1 × 0.2 × 0.3 = 0.006 m³ **[1]**

Density = 13.5 ÷ 0.006 **[1]**

= 2250 kg/m³ **[1]**

Pages 124-131: Determine

Complete the example

2. Bb **Bb**

bb bb

= $\frac{1}{2}$

3. **a)** Mean rate of reaction = change in mass ÷ **time**

= **0.2** ÷ 20 = **0.01 g/s**

b) **80** seconds

Exam practice questions

1. C_nH_{2n+2} **[1]**

2. Mass number 4 **[1]**

Atomic number 2 **[1]**

3. W = m × g

= 10 × 10 **[1]**

= 100 N **[2]**

4. 14 + 20 **[1]**

= 34% **[1]**

5. Caravan site **[1]**

will have to be closed from June onwards. **[1]**

6. *Accept any value over 600 candelas.* **[1]**

7. The percentage of gravestones with lichens in town P is 17%, in Q it is 20% and in R it is 25% / Most lichens on graves stones in R, then Q and then P. **[2]**

Therefore, town P contains the most pollution as lichens are more likely to die. **[1]**

8. **a)** Metal **[1]**

b) °C **[1]**

c) *Most reactive to least reactive:* Calcium, cobalt, copper (*Accept* Ca, Co and Cu) **[1]**

9. **a)** *Accept any number in the range of 24–26°C* **[1]**

b) At 80°C 170 g of potassium nitrate **[1]**

At 50°C 80g of potassium nitrate **[1]**

170 - 80 = 90 g potassium nitrate crystals formed **[1]**

10. Time = 1 hour = 1 x 60 x 60 = 3600 s [1]
    Distance = speed x time [1]
    Distance = 40 x 3600 = 144 000 m [1]
    = 144 km. [1]
11. F = k × e so k = F ÷ e [1]
    F = m × g = 5 × 10 = 50 N [1]
    k = 50 N ÷ 0.1 m = 500 N/m [2]
12. Object A – No [1]
    Object B – Yes [1]
    Object C – Yes [1]

Pages 132-137: Calculate

Complete the example
2. $s = d \div t$
   $s = 100 \text{ m} \div 5$
   $s = \textbf{20 m/s}$
3. a) Surface area = 24
      Volume = 8
      Ratio = **3 : 1**
   b) $1 \div 36 = \textbf{0.027 777 77}$
      = **0.028** / second

Exam practice questions
1. a) 100 – (42 + 44 + 10) = 100 – 96 = 4% [1]
   b) (67 × 44) ÷ 100 [1]
      = 29.48 million [1]
2. a) 75% [1]
   b) 25% of 800 [1]
      = 200 [1]
3. P = V × I
   = 240 × 5 [1]
   = 1200 **[1]** W **[1]**
4. a) 1 μm = 1000 nm [1]
      1000 ÷ 100
      = 10 times [1]
   b) One order of magnitude [1]
5. 12 + (2 × 16) = 44 [1]
6. Quantity of product formed = 404.80 – 403.65 = 1.15 g [1]
   Mean rate of reaction = quantity of product formed ÷ time
   or
   Mean rate of reaction = 1.15 ÷ 90 = 0.012 777 78 [1]
   = 0.0128 **[1]** g/s **[1]**
7. 23 x 2 = 46 [1]
   46 + 16 = 62 [1]
8. a = (v – u) ÷ t [1]
   = (50 – 0) ÷ 10 [1]
   = 5 **[1]** m/s² **[1]**
9. V = I × R [1]
   I = V ÷ R [1]
   I = 10 ÷ 100 = 0.1 **[1]** A **[1]**
10. E = P × t [1]
    t = 3600 s E = 18 × 3600 [1]
    = 64 800 J = 64.8 kJ [1]

11. Kinetic energy = 0.5 x mass x (speed)² [1]
    = 0.5 x 15 000 x 10² [1]
    = 7500 x 100 [1]
    = 750 000 [1]

Pages 138-139: Balance

Complete the example
2. $N_2 + 3H_2 \rightleftharpoons 2NH_3$

Exam practice questions
1. $4Li + O_2 \rightarrow 2Li_2O$ [1]
2. $C_2H_5OH + 3O_2 \rightarrow 2CO_2 + 3H_2O$ [1]
3. $2NH_4OH + H_2SO_4 \rightarrow (NH_4)_2SO_4 + 2H_2O$ [1]
4. $Na_2CO_3 + 2HCl \rightarrow 2NaCl + CO_2 + H_2O$ [1]

Pages 140-145: Measure

Complete the example
2. White blood cell = 26 mm and red blood cell = **13 mm**
   Ratio = **2 : 1**

Exam practice questions
1. 35°C [1]
2. 50 cm³ (Accept 51 cm³) [1]
3. Width of pore = 4 mm [1]
   4 mm = 4000 μm [1]
   Magnification = ×40 [1]
4. a) 42 mm (accept +/– 1) [1]
   b) 0.168 mm (accept answer to a) divided by 250) [1]
   c) 168 μm [1]
5. 50 ÷ 0 1 [1]
   = 500 times [1]
6. 15 ÷ 0.03 [1]
   = 500 times [1]
7. 126.6887 g [1]
   126.6887 ÷ 1000 = 0.1266887 kg [1]
   =0.13 kg [1]
8. 51 cm³ [1]

Pages 146-153: Plan

Complete the example
2. Set up three beakers, each one wrapped up in a different insulation material. The same thickness of material should be used in each case and should be applied in the same way. Place a thermometer in each beaker. Heat some water to a temperature of, e.g., 50°C. Add the same volume of water to each beaker and record the temperature of the water in each beaker. After e.g., 10 minutes, record the temperature of the water in each beaker.

Calculate the temperature change in each beaker and relate to the insulation material used.

3. Add the same mass and **surface area** of metals to the same **volume** and concentration of (dilute) nitric acid. Observe the temperature change or the number of **bubbles**.

Determine conclusion:
- Silver has no reaction.
- Zinc has some bubbles and **an increase** in temperature.
- Calcium has **lots of bubbles** and the **greatest increase** in temperature.

Exam practice questions

1. Use the measuring cylinder to measure 100 cm³ / the same volume of each sample of water. **[1]**
   Put the sample of water into the evaporating basin. Measure the mass of the evaporating basin and water sample. **[1]**
   Evaporate / boil / heat the water. Allow basin to cool. **[1]**
   Measure the mass of the evaporating basin and salts. Calculate the mass of dissolved salts (mass of evaporating basin with water sample – mass of evaporating basin with salt). **[1]**
   Repeat (method for each water sample). **[1]**
   Calculate an average / mean mass of dissolved salts per sample. **[1]**

2.

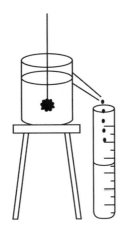

   Suspend the object from a thread. **[1]**
   Set up a Eureka can or beaker so it is full of water and any overflow / displacement will be captured by a measuring cylinder. **[1]**
   Carefully lower the object into the water and record the volume of the water displaced. **[1]**
   The volume of the water displaced is equivalent to the volume of the solid. **[1]**

3. Measure the distance between the lamp and the beaker. **[1]**
   Count the number of bubbles given off by the pondweed in a certain time. **[1]**
   Repeat the reading and calculate a mean / average. **[1]**

Repeat this for different distances between the lamp and the beaker. **[1]**
Make sure that the pondweed is left for a while before taking each reading. **[1]**
Convert the distances into light intensities using $1/d^2$. **[1]**

4. Use three or more people. **[1]**
   Measure reaction time for left and right hand of each person. **[1]**
   Use ruler drop test / computer programme to measure reaction time. **[1]**
   Repeat reaction time test for each hand. Remove any anomalous readings. **[1]**
   Calculate the mean reaction time for each hand. **[1]**
   Use similar people (similar age, same gender, same time of day, same amount of food / drink / rest, same dominant hand). **[1]**

5. Cut a piece of chromatography paper into a rectangle that can easily fit into a beaker. **[1]**
   Then use a pencil to draw a line about 1 cm from the bottom. Put a dot of the red dye on the pencil line. **[1]**
   Add just under 1 cm depth of solvent to the beaker and insert the paper so the edge of the paper is touching the solvent. **[1]**
   When the solvent line is near the top, remove the paper and use a pencil to mark the solvent front. Allow the chromatogram to dry. **[1]**
   Measure the distance from the start line to the centre of every spot on the chromatogram and the distance from the start line to the solvent front. **[1]**
   Use these measurements to calculate the Rf value for every substance in the red dye. **[1]**

6. Add excess copper(II) oxide to sulfuric acid.
   Stir. **[1]**
   Filter off the excess copper(II) oxide. **[1]**
   Collect the filtrate. **[1]**
   Heat to half the volume. **[1]**
   Allow to crystallise. **[1]**
   Remove crystals and pat dry with absorbent paper / Put in a drying oven. **[1]**

7. Fill the eureka can/displacement can with water. **[1]**
   Carefully lower the irregular object into the water and collect the water that runs out. **[1]**
   Measure the volume of the displaced water using a measuring cylinder. **[1]**
   Use a top pan balance to measure the mass in grams of the rock. **[1]**
   Calculate the density **[1]**
   by dividing the mass by the volume. **[1]**

8. Set up the length of wire on a ruler connected to a voltmeter (in parallel), an ammeter (in series), a power supply and a switch. **[1]**
   Clip the wire in place. **[1]**
   Decide on the lengths to be investigated and for each of these lengths adjust the distance between the connections

to the rest of the circuit so that the correct length of the wire being tested is part of the circuit. **[1]**

Record the length of the wire being tested that is in the circuit, the potential difference across the ends of that length and the current flowing through it. **[1]**

For each set of readings, divide the potential difference by the current to get the resistance. **[1]**

A graph can then be drawn of length of wire against resistance. **[1]**

Pages 154–159: Design

Complete the example

2. Use a **quadrat** to sample the penalty areas.

Place the **quadrats at random**.

Count the number of **dandelions in the quadrats**.

Measure the **area** of the penalty areas and calculate the **total number of dandelions**.

Repeat this process for the **rest of the pitch**.

Compare the numbers from the penalty areas and the rest of the pitch.

Exam practice questions

1. Set up a circuit with one lamp, an ammeter, a power supply / battery and some connecting wires. **[1]**
   Record the current reading on the ammeter. **[1]**
   Now add a second lamp, **[1]**
   read the ammeter and record these. **[1]**
   Repeat this, having added additional lamps and recording the current. **[1]**
   The number of lamps can now be compared to the current to see what the pattern is between the figures. **[1]**

2. Set the ramp up, measure the vertical height of the top of the ramp and the horizontal length of the ramp. **[1]**
   Divide the height by the length to get the gradient. **[1]**
   Use a stopwatch to time the car rolling from top to bottom of the ramp. Repeat this a couple of times and if any of the readings are significantly different then repeat them. **[1]**

   Alter the height of the ramp and repeat the readings for the new height, calculating the gradient and recording the values. **[1]**

3. Divide a large group of people into two smaller groups. The people in each group should be the same age, sex and not have consumed any other drugs. This makes the results of the investigation valid. **[1]**
   One group is given cola to drink but the other is the control group. **[1]**
   Test the reaction time for each person in each group. This can be done by dropping a ruler between their thumb and first finger. **[1]**
   When they trap it, then measure the distance from the starting point. **[1]**

This measurement can be converted into a reaction time. **[1]**
Calculate a mean / average result for each group and compare the two groups. **[1]**

4. Add water to the cheese, then grind / mix to make a food solution. Decant / filter the food solution from the cheese into a test tube. **[1]**
   Add Biuret's solution (mixture of potassium hydroxide solution and copper(II) sulfate solution) to the food sample. **[1]**
   Stir for two minutes and the solution should change colour from blue to purple indicating the presence of protein. **[1]**
   Put a sample of cheese on a white tile / in a test tube.
   Add a drop of iodine solution. No colour change as no starch present. **[1]**

5. Make a warm water bath (35°C). Put the containers of starch solution, amylase enzyme and pH buffer onto the warm bath. **[1]**
   Add two drops of iodine solution into each spot of a spotting tile. Add the same volume of amylase enzyme, starch and pH buffer into the same test tube. **[1]**
   Mix the solution in the test tube and place into warm water bath. Start the stop watch. **[1]**
   Repeat until the iodine solution has no observable change. Record the time this takes. Repeat with different pH buffers. **[1]**

6. Use a balance to measure the mass of the bolt and record this. **[1]**
   Suspend the bolt from a piece of thread. Set up a measuring cylinder that the bolt will fit into and put water into the cylinder. **[1]**
   The water level should be around half full. The volume of water should be measured and recorded. **[1]**
   Lower the bolt on the thread into the water, ensure it is completely immersed and read the new volume. **[1]**
   Subtract the old volume from the new one to get the volume of the bolt. **[1]**
   Divide the mass of the bolt by its volume to get the density. **[1]**

7. Students should work in groups. One person could be the tester, another the person the test is carried out on and the third the recorder. **[1]**
   The tester holds a 30 cm ruler vertically by the top end and the person being tested has their hand poised by the bottom end. The tester lets go and the person being tested grasps it as soon as they see it start to fall. The reading on the ruler where it is grasped is recorded. **[1]**
   Repeat this several times, record the values and eliminate any outliers. **[1]**
   The person being tested should then drink a serving of an energy drink, wait a few minutes and be tested again. **[1]**
   The average reaction time before and after taking the drink should be calculated. **[1]**
   Groups should then compare their data to see what the overall trend is. **[1]**

Pages 160-167: Plot

Complete the example

2.

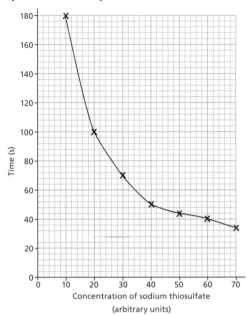

2.

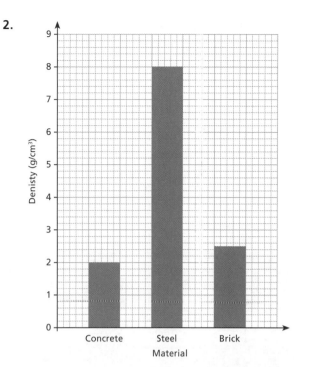

[1]

3.

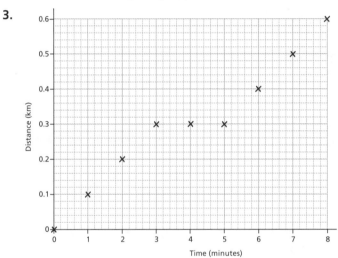

3.

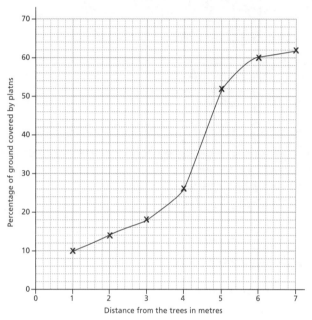

Correct y-axis scale [1]
Correct x-axis scale [1]
Correct plotting of data +/– 2 squares [2]
Line of best fit [1]

Exam practice questions

1.

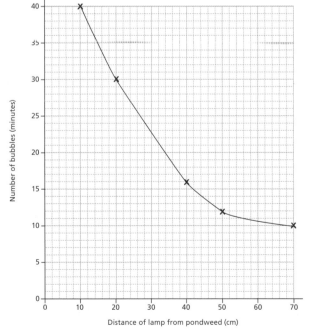

5 correct plots [2]
Smooth curve for line of best fit [1]

4. *All points plotted correctly as shown (+/– 2 small squares). (Allow 1 mark if five or six points are correctly plotted.)* **[2]**

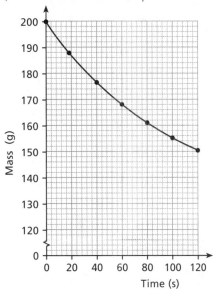

5.

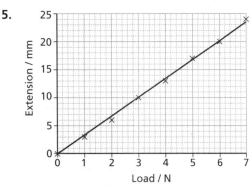

y-axis label including units **[1]**
y-axis appropriate scale **[1]**
Correct plotting of data +/- 2 squares accuracy **[2]**

Pages 168-175: Compare

Complete the example

2. Covalent bonds are stronger than intermolecular forces.

3. Both of these reactions supply energy for **muscle contraction**.
They are both **exothermic** reactions and use **glucose**.
Aerobic respiration needs **oxygen**, but anaerobic respiration does not.
Anaerobic respiration produces **lactic acid**, but aerobic respiration produces **carbon dioxide**.
Less energy is released by anaerobic respiration.

Exam practice questions

1. The line of best fit for a higher surface area would have a steeper slope.

2. Both methods will power the calculator and enable it to be used **[1]**
but the photovoltaic cells are dependent on light, which the battery isn't. **[1]**
This means the calculator with photovoltaic cells is free to run but depends on light **[1]**

whereas a battery powered calculator will need the batteries recharging or replacing. **[1]**

3. Both involve current flowing through a circuit. But the direct flow means that the current is always flowing in one direction **[1]**
whereas the alternating current means that the direction of current flow keeps changing. **[1]**

4. Both types of transformers have two sets of coils and both transform the ac voltage from one level to another. But the step up transformer has more turns on the secondary coil than the primary, increasing the voltage, **[1]**
whereas the step down has more turns on the primary coil than the secondary, decreasing the voltage. **[1]**

5. AIDS is caused by a virus (HIV) but gonorrhoea is caused by a bacterium. **[1]**
Both are spread by sexual contact. **[1]**
HIV leads to AIDS and is spread by using infected needles. **[1]**
Both can be prevented by using condoms during sexual activity. **[1]**
AIDS can be treated by the use of antivirals and gonorrhoea by antibiotics. **[1]**

6. Both are methods of cell division. **[1]**
They both require DNA to be replicated first. **[1]**
Meiosis halves the number of chromosomes but mitosis keeps the same number. **[1]**
Meiosis produces cells that are genetically different but mitosis produces genetically identical cells. **[1]**
Meiosis produces gametes but mitosis produces body cells. **[1]**

7. Active transport requires energy. Osmosis is passive / does not require energy. **[1]**
Active transport moves against the concentration gradient / moves minerals from low to high concentrations. **[1]**
Osmosis moves water with the concentration gradient from high concentration of water (dilute solutions) to low concentration of water (concentrated solutions). **[1]**
Osmosis and active transport both happen across a membrane. **[1]**

8. Both of these reactions supply energy for muscle contraction. **[1]**
They are both exothermic reactions and use glucose. **[1]**
Aerobic respiration needs oxygen, but anaerobic respiration does not. **[1]**
Anaerobic respiration produces lactic acid, but aerobic respiration produces carbon dioxide (and water). **[1]**
Less energy is released by anaerobic respiration. **[1]**

9. *Four points from:* All contain only carbon atoms; All contain covalent bonds; All saturated (only contain single bonds); Diamond and graphite are giant covalent structures; Buckminsterfullerene is a simple molecule; Graphite and buckminsterfullerene have three covalent bonds on every carbon atom, whereas diamond has four covalent bonds on every carbon atom; Graphite has layers (planes) of atoms that can easily slide, whereas diamond and buckminsterfullerene do not; Graphite has electrons that are free to move, whereas diamond and buckminsterfullerene do not; Buckminsterfullerene makes a 3D cage, whereas graphite and diamond do not. **[4]**

10. Both ethane and pentane are small molecules where the atoms are held together by covalent bonds **[1]** with intermolecular forces of attraction between the molecules. **[1]**

Pentane is a bigger molecule and so has a higher melting point and boiling point **[1]**

meaning that pentane is a liquid at room temperature, whereas ethane is a gas. **[1]**

Both pentane and ethane are hydrocarbons as they contain only hydrogen and carbon. **[1]**

They can be used as fuels and undergo combustion to make carbon, carbon monoxide, carbon dioxide and water. **[1]**

11. *Any six points from:* Fresh water only: plentiful and easy supply; fewer treatment steps; quicker to process. Sewage water only: more difficult to collect; more treatment steps; slower process; sedimentation (produce sewage sludge and effluent); aerobic biological digestion of effluent (reduces solid waste); sludge anaerobically digested (to remove organic matter). Both fresh water and sewage water: filtered / screening and grit removal to remove insoluble solids; sterilised (UV, chlorine, ozone treated). **[6]**

Pages 176-183: Estimate

Complete the example

2. *Best straight line drawn.*
Vertical line drawn down from the line at 200 beats per minute.
Correct reading of speed from the x-axis (approximately 48 km/h).

3. The percentage submerged is the amount of the whole **block** that is under the surface of the **water**. By comparing this with the **total**, this will be around **80**%.

Exam practice questions

1. *Accept any number between –41 and 25°C.* **[1]**
2. *14° (+/–2°)* **[1]**
3. $\dfrac{18 \times 10}{4}$ **[1]**
   = 45 **[1]**
4. The mean number of larvae per quadrat = (12 + 10 + 7 + 11) ÷ 4 = 10 **[1]**
   Estimated total number of larvae = (10 × 12) ÷ 0.25 **[1]**
   = 480 **[1]**
5. Area of the field = 50 × 100 = 5000 m² **[1]**
   5000 × 6.2 = 31 000 buttercup plants **[1]**

6. *Accept any number less than 1.* **[1]**
7. *Accept a number between –119 and 24°C.* **[1]**
8. **a)** *Accept a number between 85% and 90%* **[1]**
   b) *Accept an answer between $\frac{1}{9}$ and $\frac{1}{13}$* **[1]**
9. 1.1 cm *(+/–0.2)* **[1]**
10. –150° *(+/–10°)* **[1]**
11. *Accept answer between 0.50 V and 0.57 V* **[1]**
12. 2.8 cm **[1]**

Pages 184-189: Predict

Complete the example

2. Grey / Black solid

Exam practice questions

1. **a)** Changes colour / Becomes covered in a rose coloured solid **[1]**
   b) From blue **[1]**
   to colourless **[1]**
2. **a)** Slow reaction, where the metal slowly changes to a darker colour. **[1]**
   b) Iron(III) chloride (*Accept* iron chloride) **[1]**
3. 80 seconds **[1]**
   = 1 minute and 20 seconds **[1]**
   = 1.33 minutes **[1]**
4. **a)** It will increase the rate of reaction. **[1]**
   b) The same maximum mass will be produced. **[1]**
   c) It will increase the rate of reaction. **[1]**
5. The particles collide more often in a given amount of time **[1]**
   the particles have more energy / more have the activation energy **[1]**
6. The cup without the lid will cool down quicker **[1]**
   as convection currents above the surface of the coffee are free to transfer energy to the surroundings. **[1]**
7. The oil will be on top **[1]**
   as it is less dense. **[1]**
8. *The new line should have a gentler gradient and start to level out (though not curve downwards).* **[1]**

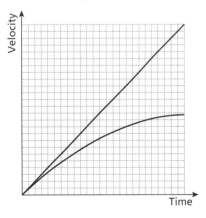

This shows that the increase of velocity will become less as it nears (and possibly reaches) its terminal velocity. **[1]**

Pages 190-197: Evaluate

Complete the example

2. Carbon and **aluminium** are cheaper reactants than hydrogen, which **is the most expensive**. However, there is a financial and time cost for removing a solid product such as **aluminium oxide** from the zinc, which is not needed when **carbon** or **hydrogen** are used. So, **using carbon to reduce zinc oxide** would be the best method.

3. The model is an effective one because it shows that charged particles originate in the circuit and don't all start from **the battery**. It also shows that these particles all set off in motion **at the same time**. The model shows that the current flow is the same **everywhere in the circuit**. If one of the pupils starts to grip the cord harder, their hand will get warmer due to friction and this shows how **resistance works**. However, the model only works for a series **circuit** and it is also inaccurate because **it doesn't show how charge is transferred**. Overall, the value of the model is **partial**.

Exam practice questions

1. The two important things are the amount of energy which has to be transferred to the lamp and the life expectancy. **[1]**
   The data shows that of the three types of lamp the LED lasts for much longer **[1]**
   and uses the least amount of energy. **[1]**
   The other factor could be the cost of the lamp but we are not told that so on the basis of this information it is the LED lamp which should be selected. **[1]**

2. The graph supports the claim because the men with heart disease have on average narrower coronary arteries. **[1]**
   This means that less blood will reach the heart muscle, **[1]**
   making heart disease more likely. **[1]**
   However, the graph shows that there is an overlap in results between the two groups. **[1]**
   Also, the trial had a small sample size and only tested men, so the results may not apply to all people. **[1]**

3. Number of deaths has increased as margarine eaten increases while butter eaten decreases. **[1]**
   Then as margarine eaten decreases, the number of deaths decreases. **[1]**
   However, the increase in deaths starts before butter or margarine consumption changes. **[1]**
   A correlation does not mean a cause / there could be other factors causing the change in death rate. **[1]**
   Only data about heart disease is given in the graphs, so cannot say butter is healthier. **[1]**
   The effect of high butter consumption may take time to be seen as it may cause deaths from heart disease in the future. **[1]**

4. *Evaluation to include five of these points:*
   Both glass and plastic are finite resources; Both glass and plastic can be fully recycled a number of times; Lower temperature is used to produce plastic; Glass is re-used; Glass contains more recycled materials; Glass bottles are heavier than plastic bottles, using more fossil fuels to transport them; Glass is more brittle than plastic and bottles are more likely to get damaged leading to loss of product;
   Plus one of the following judgements:
   Judgement for glass being the more sustainable:
   - Glass is a more sustainable material to make drinks bottles as it is more likely to be reused and recycled than plastic bottles.
   Judgement for plastic being more sustainable:
   - Plastic is the more sustainable material as it uses less fossil fuel during its lifespan. If the bottles could be reused and the percentage of recycled material increased in the bottle, it would be even more sustainable. **[6]**

5. *Evaluation should include six of these points:*
   Bicycle C produces the most CO_2 during manufacture; Bicycle B produces the most CO_2 per km when being used; Bicycle C produces the most CO_2 from manufacture and being used for 1000 km; Bicycle B produces the most CO_2 from manufacture and being used for the average lifetime of the bicycle; Bicycle A produces least CO_2 during manufacture and is a push bike, meaning the least amount of CO_2 generated over the lifetime; Bicycles B and C are e-bikes so they emit CO_2 during use; Bicycle C produces most CO_2 during manufacture, but less CO_2 than bicycle B when being used; Bicycle A has the least carbon footprint of all the bicycles; If you wanted an e-bike then bicycle B has a smaller carbon footprint in the short term but bicycle C has a lower carbon footprint over the whole lifetime of the bicycle. **[6]**

6. This method would record evidence to be analysed. **[1]**
   The students could study the video and use the markings to see how far the trolley had travelled in each interval. **[1]**
   They could see how many seconds it took to cover each of the 10 cm sections of the journey. **[1]**
   Unless they move the phone along in the direction the trolley is moving, it won't be directly above the markings, which may introduce errors into the data. **[1]**
   If the trolley is moving quickly the motion could be blurred. **[1]**
   Overall it is a good way as long as the trolley's speed is kept low, the phone is moved along above the ramp and repeat measurements are taken. **[1]**

Pages 198-203: Justify

Complete the example

2. Most of the **alpha particles** went straight through the gold foil. This means they did not hit anything with mass and so the **atom** must be mainly empty space.
   Some of the alpha particles **changed direction**, and some **reflected back**. This must mean they were **repelled** by a like charge. But as this only happened occasionally, we can conclude there is a **positive centre** to the nucleus and this must be where most of the particles or mass is found in the atom.

3. a) Repeat readings are important because **there are reasons why the value obtained could vary**. There might be a slight pause in releasing the vehicle, an error in measuring **the time** or the vehicle might change **direction** slightly.

   b) The first three readings are **very close** to each other with small gaps between, but the **final reading** is significantly different with a much **bigger** gap. Taking the **mean** of the other three will give an answer nearer to the true value.

Exam practice questions

1. *Any four points from:*
   The cell has a cytoplasm and a cell membrane surrounded by a cell wall; The genetic material is not enclosed in a nucleus/No nucleus; Has a single DNA loop;
   Has two small rings of DNA / plasmids; Prokaryotic cell;
   This cell is a prokaryotic cell as it has no nucleus and therefore is an example of a bacterium. **[4]**

2. *Any three points from:* To accurately identify species; To collect data about ecosystems and populations; It allows comparison between living things based on recognisable features; It implies how closely related different species are; It allows for easy sorting of data; Predictions about a species can be made because of the name; Scientists are not confused as to which living thing someone is describing. **[3]**

3. a) Magnesium has a very slow rate of reaction with water. **[1]**
   No bubbles are observed. **[1]**
   Control is used to compare what would happen if there was no acid. **[1]**
   So, control would be pure water. **[1]**

   b) A, D, C, B **[1]**
   The greater the number of bubbles, the higher the reactivity. **[1]**
   A has the most bubbles, then D, then C, and B has no bubbles. **[1]**

4. *Any four points from:*
   Ionic compounds make giant lattices;
   Ionic compounds / giant structures / lattices need a lot of energy to change state;
   Both B and C have high melting and boiling points / cannot be A as melting and boiling point too low;

Ionic compounds can only conduct electricity when molten or dissolved in water / in aqueous solution / when ions are free to move;
Only substance B has both a high melting and boiling point as well as not conducting when a solid, but conducts when in aqueous solutions. **[4]**

5. Both designs are likely to keep the drink hot (hot drink) or cold (cold drink) as they are good insulators. B is likely to be better as a vacuum is an excellent insulator. **[1]**
   A is made from cheaper materials so won't cost as much. **[1]**
   A is made from less robust materials so probably won't last as long. **[1]**
   Overall B would be a good choice: it may cost more, but will last longer, insulate better and is recyclable. **[1]**

6. The ohmmeter is quicker and easier to set up so it is less likely there will be faults in the circuit. **[1]**
   The ohmmeter gives a resistance reading directly, therefore no opportunities for errors. **[1]**
   Easy to take repeat readings to check the value. **[1]**

Pages 204-223: Mixed Questions

1. a) X = pituitary **[1]**
      Y = pancreas **[1]**
      Z = ovary **[1]**

   b) *Any two from:* Hormonal response is slower / more general / lasts longer; Hormonal response involves chemicals but nervous response uses electrical impulses. **[2]**

2. a) Ovulation **[1]**
   b) FSH **[1]**
   c) Day 21 **[1]**

3. a) oxygen **[1]**
      and glucose **[1]**
   b) 17.5 *(allow 17–18)* **[1]**
   c) 6 arbitrary units **[1]**

4. a) Root hair cell **[1]**
   b) Cell wall **[1]**
   c) C **[1]**

5. a)

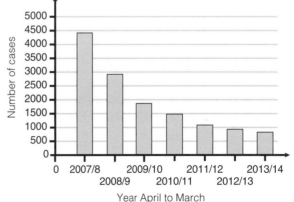

   Bar must be drawn to correct height. **[1]**
   b) 80% **[1]**

c) A mutation causes a bacterium to become resistant. **[1]**
Sensitive bacteria are killed by the antibiotic. **[1]**
The resistant bacteria reproduce quickly until all the population is resistant. **[1]**

6. a) oxygen + glucose **[1]** carbon dioxide + water **[1]**

b)

c) As intensity increases, breathing rate increases. **[1]**

7. a) White blood cells **[1]**
recognise the pathogen **[1]**
and produce antibodies **[1]**
quickly. **[1]**

b) $420 \div 531 \times 100 = 79.09\%$ **[1]**
Percentage = 79% **[1]**

c) By air **[1]**

d) *Any one from:* Sexual contact; Contact with body fluids / blood; Sharing needles **[1]**

e) They are caused by viruses that live inside cells. **[1]**
Drugs that kill the virus would also damage cells. **[1]**
Viruses are not destroyed by antibiotics. **[1]**

8. a) Homozygous **[1]**

b) $1800 \div 585 = 3.076 = 3.08 : 1$ *(to 2 decimal places)* **[1]**

c) 23 **[1]**

d) Testes **[1]**

e) Female, because the egg always donates X **[1]**
therefore offspring will have XX, which is female. **[1]**

f) Mitosis **[1]**

g) Egg / ovum and pollen **[1]**

9. a) Life cycle assessment / analysis **[1]**

b) The style of the clothing **[1]**

10. a) X = condenser **[1]**
Y = (round bottom) flask **[1]**

b) At X the water vapour condenses to form liquid water. **[1]**
At Y the liquid water evaporates / boils to form water vapour. **[1]**

11. a) The forces between the rubidium ions and the delocalised electrons are weaker than the forces between the potassium ions and the delocalised electrons. **[1]**

b) The ions cannot move. **[1]**

12. a) 11 **[1]**

b) neutron **[1]**
proton **[1]**

c) An isotope has a different number of neutrons. **[1]**

13. a) C_3H_8 **[1]**

b) Propane **[1]**

c) Water **[1]**
Carbon dioxide **[1]**

14. a) Number of protons = 15 **[1]**
Number of neutrons = 16 **[1]**
Number of electrons = 15 **[1]**

b) It has five electrons in its outer shell. **[1]**

15. a) It helps them to compare products / services **[1]**

b) *Any suitable answer, such as* price; size; cost to run **[1]**

c) How much of the car can be recycled. **[1]**

d) Environmental impact of paper – *any two from:* Paper is made from trees; More trees can be planted; Trees are renewable; Paper is biodegradable **[2]**
Environmental impact of plastic – *any two from:* Plastics are made from oil; Oil is a non-renewable source; Plastic is non-biodegradable; Plastic bags can be used more times; Plastic bags do not dissolve in water and have to be thrown away **[2]**

16. a) Forces A & C and B & D cancel each other out. **[1]**

b) D **[1]**

c)

[1]

d) A **[1]**

e) C **[1]**

f) mean speed = distance ÷ time
= $840\,000 \div 120$ **[1]**
= 7000 **[1]**

17. a) Density = mass ÷ volume / p = m ÷ v **[1]**

b) $2400 \div 0.8$ **[1]**
= 3000 kg / m³ **[2]**

18. a) Light-dependent resistor /LDR **[1]**

b) 7 kilo-ohms **[1]**

c) V = IR
$V = 0.0003 \times 7000$ **[1]**
= 2.1 V **[1]**

19. a) *Gradient indicated*
$y \div x$
$= 20 \div 300$ **[1]**
= 0.067 **[1]**

b) $\Delta E = mc\Delta\theta = Pt$
$mc[\Delta\theta] \div t = P$ **[1]**
$c = P \div (m \times \text{gradient})$
$= 54 \div (1.5 \times 0.0428)$ **[1]**
= 840.5 J / kg / °C **[1]**

20. a)

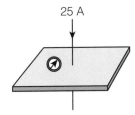

25 A

*The arrow should be pointing upwards and at an angle
as shown.* **[1]**

b) Current in a wire produces a magnetic field **[1]**
The plotting compass interacts with the circular
magnetic field around the wire. **[1]**

c)

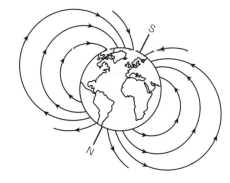

Matching field lines from N to S. **[1]**
*Lines are further apart the further they are from the
Earth.* **[1]**

21. a) 1.5 waves in 0.5 s **[1]**
3 Hz **[1]**

b) **[1]**

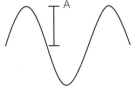

A

c) $v = f\lambda$
$\lambda = v \div f$
$= 90 \div 3$ **[1]**
$= 30$ m **[1]**

22. a) Alpha **[1]**, Beta **[1]**, Gamma **[1]**

b) There is a risk of radiation contaminating them /
getting on the skin. **[1]**
The radiation / alpha and beta particles are easily
stopped by a barrier / the clothing. **[1]**

c) There is natural background radiation present. **[1]**

d) $^{0}_{-1}e$ **[1]**

e) $^{215}_{84}Po$ **[1]**
[1]

f) Their research needs to be checked by other
scientists **[1]**
to ensure it is accurate / repeatable. **[1]**

Notes

Notes

Notes

Notes

Notes

Notes

Acknowledgements

The author and publisher are grateful to the copyright holders for permission to use quoted materials and images. Every effort has been made to trace copyright holders and obtain their permission for the use of copyright material. The author and publisher will gladly receive information enabling them to rectify any error or omission in subsequent editions. All facts are correct at time of going to press.

All images ©Shutterstock and HarperCollins*Publishers*

Published by Collins
An imprint of HarperCollins*Publishers* Limited
1 London Bridge Street, London SE1 9GF

HarperCollins*Publishers*
Macken House, 39/40 Mayor Street Upper
Dublin 1, D01 C9W8, Ireland

© HarperCollins*Publishers* Limited 2023

ISBN 978-0-00-864740-7

First published 2023

10 9 8 7 6 5 4 3 2 1

British Library Cataloguing in Publication Data.

A CIP record of this book is available from the British Library.

Publisher: Katie Sergeant
Authors: Ian Honeysett, Sam Holyman and Ed Walsh
Commissioning and Development: Richard Toms
Project Management: Katie Galloway
Inside Concept Design: Ian Wrigley and Sarah Duxbury
Layout: Rose & Thorn Creative Services Ltd and Ian Wrigley
Cover Design: Sarah Duxbury
Production: Bethany Brohm
Printed in the United Kingdom

MIX
Paper | Supporting responsible forestry
FSC™ C007454

This book contains FSC™ certified paper and other controlled sources to ensure responsible forest management.

For more information visit: www.harpercollins.co.uk/green